Great World Writers

TWENTIETH CENTURY

EDITOR
PATRICK M. O'NEIL

Volume 5

Hermann Hesse • Aldous Huxley

Eugène Ionesco • James Joyce • Franz Kafka

Ghassan Kanafani • Yasunari Kawabata • Nikos Kazantzakis

M.B. SMILEY LIBRARY

MARSHALL CAVENDISH
NEW YORK • TORONTO • LONDON • SYDNEY

Marshall Cavendish
99 White Plains Road
Tarrytown, New York 10591-9001

Website: www.marshallcavendish.com

Project Editor: Marian Armstrong
Development Editor: Thomas McCarthy
Editorial Director: Paul Bernabeo
Production Manager: Michael Esposito

Designer: Patrice Sheridan

Photo Research: Anne Burns Images
Carousel Research, Inc.
Laurie Platt Winfrey
Elizabeth Meryman
Van Bucher
Cristian Peña

Indexing: AEIOU
Cynthia Crippen

Library of Congress Cataloging-in-Publication Data

Great world writers : twentieth century / editor, Patrick M. O'Neil.
p. cm.
Vol. 13 is an index volume.
Includes bibliographical references and index.
ISBN 0-7614-7469-2 (v. 1)—ISBN 0-7614-7470-6 (v. 2)—
ISBN 0-7614-7471-4 (v. 3)—ISBN 0-7614-7472-2 (v. 4)—
ISBN 0-7614-7473-0 (v. 5)—ISBN 0-7614-7474-9
(v. 6)—ISBN 0-7614-7475-7 (v. 7)—ISBN 0-7614-7476-5
(v. 8)—ISBN 0-7614-7477-3 (v. 9)—ISBN 0-7614-7478-1
(v. 10)—ISBN 0-7614-7479-X (v. 11)—ISBN 0-7614-7480-3
(v. 12)—ISBN 0-7614-7481-1 (v. 13—ISBN 0-7614-7468-4 (set)
  1. Literature—20th century—Bio-bibliography—Dictionaries.
  2. Authors—20th century—Biography—Dictionaries.
  3. Literature—20th century—History and criticism. I.
O'Neil, Patrick M.

PN771.G73 2004
809'.04—dc21
[B]   2003040922

Printed in China

09 08 07 06 05 04   6 5 4 3 2 1

Contents

Hermann Hesse

BORN: July 2, 1877, Calw, Germany
DIED: August 9, 1962, Montagnola, Switzerland
IDENTIFICATION: German author and poet whose works incorporated both his strong spiritual values and his sense of the conflict between the rational and the spiritual aspects of humanity.

SIGNIFICANCE: Hesse's writings, which are characterized by rare beauty of language and command of style, introduced elements of Eastern thought, particularly of India. His familiarity with Eastern thought came to him in part through his family background and in part from his own travels to the East. His emphasis on Eastern mysticism and on the development of the individual spirit has been at the root of cycles of popular interest, especially among the young, throughout the twentieth century. Hesse was winner of the Nobel Prize for literature in 1946.

The Writer's Life

Hermann Hesse was born July 2, 1877, in the Black Forest town of Calw in southern Germany. Like many of the outstanding men of letters of nineteenth-century Germany—Jean Paul (Johann Paul Friedrich Richter), Friedrich Nietzsche, and Albert Schweitzer—Hesse came from a religious background. His father, Johannes, a Russian citizen, was born in Weissenstein, Estonia. Johannes was an orthodox Lutheran minister in the Pietist tradition. Hesse's mother, Marie Gundert (1842–1902), was born in Talatscheri, India. Her father was the noted Indologist Hermann Gundert, who had been a missionary there for more than twenty years and was a very active scholar and an accomplished linguist.

Hesse's father had been a Pietist missionary in Malabar, India, until poor health obliged him to return to Germany. He moved to Calw and became assistant to Hermann Gundert. There he met Marie, who also shared her father's intellectual interests, and a year later Johannes and Marie married. Hermann was their second child. The couple moved in 1880 to Basle, Switzerland, where Johannes became director of the Basle Missionary Society.

Childhood Years. Hesse's childhood might best be described as turbulent. By nature Hesse had a strong character, imbued with an earnest commitment to honesty and sincerity. When Hesse was barely six years old, his frustrated parents considered sending the child away to an institution where his unruliness could be better dealt with. He rebelled against virtually all authority and was transferred from school to school as a consequence of his rebelliousness. For Hermann school was unbearable; he suffered frequent headaches and sleepless nights and often ran away from home or was expelled from school. In 1890 he was sent to a preparatory school in the Swabian town of Göppingen, where he completed his Landexamen (admissions test). In 1891 he was placed in the seminary school in Maulbronn, where he again ran away. The following year he attended the gymnasium (high school) in Bad Cannstatt,

This portrait of the Hesse family was taken in the mid to late 1880s. From left to right are Hermann; his father, Johannes; his sister Marulla; his mother, Marie; his sister Adele; and his brother, Hans.

where he prepared for entrance into the German university. During this time the access Hesse had to his grandfather Gundert's vast library and to the wide circle of scholars in his grandparents' home was of immense importance for his intellectual development and provided solace for his sensitive nature. Hesse had by this time become a competent musician and budding poet.

In 1893 Hesse returned home to Calw, where he apprenticed in a clock workshop, but in 1895 he moved to the small university town of Tübingen and apprenticed in the Heckenhauer bookstore. While there he began writing seriously and published his first works of poetry and prose.

Hesse moved to Basle in 1899, again working in a bookshop and, after 1901, in an antiquarian bookstore. He was able to continue his readings in German literature, focusing now on Nietzsche and Gottfried Keller, and to devote more time to writing. He published a collection of some 200 poems in a book dedicated to his mother, who died before it appeared. In 1904 he published his first major success, *Peter Camenzind*. A year later he married Maria Bernoulli, whom he had met on an excursion to Italy. The royalties from *Peter Camenzind* permitted the young author to quit his job and devote himself entirely to writing.

This photograph of Hesse was taken in 1898 in Tübingen, a city in the industrial state of Baden-Württemberg in southwestern Germany. Hesse left Tübingen, where he was an apprentice in a bookstore, the following year.

Marriage and Domestic Life. Hermann and Maria chose to move away from the distractions of Basle. They found a farmhouse in the village of Gaienhofen on the Untersee, where their first child, Bruno, was born in 1905. Here Hesse composed a number of stories and poems. Their next home in the area had a large garden, which Hesse tended, and an unobstructed view of the lake. The circle of friends that developed in this new home included musicians and artists from whom Hesse drew inspiration and ideas.

During the Gaienhofen years Hesse published many new stories in journals and collections. He also became increasingly involved in writing reviews and literary criticism, embarking on a practice that he was to pursue throughout his lifetime. A second son, Heiner, was born in 1909, and a third, Martin, in 1911. Critical recognition of his work grew as he devoted himself more and more to writing in order to earn money to support his wife and children.

Hesse became restless, and his desire to travel and to learn led him in 1911 to undertake a journey to India, the land of his mother's birth, in the hope of establishing intellectual contacts there and of learning more about Indian thought and religion. The anticipated contacts did not come, much to Hesse's disappointment, but he did learn much about the land that added to his understanding of India's history and provided him with material for later writings.

In the autumn of 1912, the Hesse family moved to a new home in Bern, Switzerland. Here he published his novel *Rosshalde* in 1913. Although it did not enjoy the success of his earlier work, Hesse believed that in this work he had reached the peak of his writing skills.

World War I. At the outbreak of World War I, Hesse had been living in Switzerland for two years, but he still felt obliged, as a German citizen, to become involved on the side of his country. He contacted the German consulate in Bern to volunteer for service but was rejected. He was summoned instead to do service until 1919 with the Prisoners of War Welfare Organization (*Deutschen Kriegsgefangenenfürsorge*). Hesse's experience here strengthened his own pacifism and led him to express his objections to the evils of war in writing. Condemned in the press and denounced as a traitor, he could no longer publish his works in Germany.

Depression and Family Tragedy. Hesse's work with the prisoners of war was interrupted only by a brief pause in 1916 to recover from enormous personal burdens: His father had died that year, his youngest child had become seriously ill, and his marriage was in jeopardy. He began psychoanalysis and was able to find relief from his unrelenting depression and to return to his prisoner aid work. By 1918 his wife's health had deteriorated to the extent that she had to be placed in a mental institution. The marriage was destroyed, and at the end of the war in 1919, Hesse was forced to begin his life over again.

Writing in the Postwar Years. Unable to publish under his own name in Germany, he used the pseudonym Emil Sinclair, under which he published a number of works during

Hesse, who found great satisfaction in outdoor work, is seen here at his home in Montagnola in Lugano, Switzerland, in 1935. The photograph was taken by his third son, Martin.

HIGHLIGHTS IN HESSE'S LIFE

1877   Hermann Hesse is born July 2, the second son of Johannes Hesse and his wife, Marie (née Gundert), in Calw, Württemberg.

1881–1886 Family moves to Basle, where Johannes was teaching.

1891   Hesse attends the seminary in Maulbronn but runs away after seven months.

1891–1892 Attends Maulbronn Seminary.

1892–1893 Attends gymnasium in Bad Cannstatt.

1893–1894 Is bookshop apprentice in Calw.

1894–1895 Works as apprentice mechanic in clock workshop.

1895–1898 Apprentices in bookshop in Tübingen.

1899   First collection of verse published, *Romantische Lieder* (*Romantic Songs*), also the prose work *Eine Stunde hinter Mitternacht* (*An Hour behind Midnight*).

1899–1903 Hesse works in a bookshop in Basle.

1904   *Peter Camenzind* is published; Hesse marries Maria Bernoulli.

1906   *Unterm Rad* (*Beneath the Wheel*) is published.

1907–1912 With Albert Langen, Ludwig Thoma, and others, Hesse publishes the leftist journal *März*.

1911   Travels in Southeast Asia for several months with the painter Hans Sturzenegger; visits Ceylon, Singapore, and Sumatra.

1912   The family moves to Bern.

1914   Volunteers for military service but is rejected because of his poor vision; works instead for the Prisoners of War Welfare Organization.

1916   Psychological counseling in Lucerne.

1919   Moves with his family to Montagnola, Tessin.

1919–1922 Coedits *Vivos Voco*.

1922   *Siddhartha* appears.

1923   Becomes a Swiss citizen and divorces wife.

1924   Marries Ruth Wenger (the marriage dissolved in 1927).

1926   Is elected to the Prussian Academy of Arts.

1927   *Steppenwolf* is published.

1930   *Narcissus and Goldmund* appears.

1931   Hesse marries Ninon Dolbin, an art historian and resigns from the Prussian Academy of Arts for political reasons.

1933–1945 Avoids signing political petitions but makes clear in his writings his rejection of the rule of the National Socialist Workers Party; aids numerous artists and writers who flee Germany.

1942   Publishes his collected poetry.

1943   Publishes *The Glass Bead Game* but withdraws from further writing because of poor health.

1946   Receives Nobel Prize for literature.

1947   Receives honorary doctorate from the University of Bern.

1955   Receives peace prize of the German book trade.

1962   Dies in Montagnola on August 9.

this time. Most significant of these was *Demian* in 1919.The same year Hesse helped establish a new journal, *Vivos Voco,* in the hope of rebuilding postwar Germany through the education of Germany's youth. Hesse was coeditor of the journal for a period and continued to submit reviews for it after he ended his involvement in editing. It was also in 1919 that Hesse began work on *Siddhartha,* incorporating his years of travel in the East and his study of Indian and Chinese philosophy and religion.

In 1923 Hesse acquired Swiss citizenship, and in 1924 he married Ruth Wenger. This marriage, however, was not destined to last, and in 1927 the couple parted. Hesse had grown increasingly concerned about the role of technology in contemporary society and about the discord between the world of ideals and events in the real world. These reflections later formed the basis for his novel *Steppenwolf,* published in 1927.

The year 1927 also saw the publication of *Die Nürnberger Reise* (The Trip to Nuremberg) and the start of work on *Narziss und Goldmund* (*Narcissus and Goldmund*), which appeared in 1930. In this same year Hesse experienced physical exhaustion as a result of overwork and stress. He later resigned from the Prussian Academy on the eve of the National Socialist Party's rise to power in 1933. In the same year he remarried, taking Ninon Dolbin Ausländer as his third wife. The couple moved into Casa Rossa, a new home that a friend had built for them in Montagnola and deeded to them in perpetuity.

With the growing turmoil in Europe during the 1930s, Germany's political future became increasingly clear to Hesse, as indeed it had become to many others, but he avoided active involvement in opposing the events in Germany beyond commenting on the political evils there. He was the "onlooker," still hurting from the response to his activities during World War I.

In his final major work, *Das Glasperlenspiel* (*The Glass Bead Game*), which he had begun back in 1931, Hesse returned once again to his interest in the East and in Eastern philosophy. Because of the wartime conditions, however, it appeared only in Switzerland.

In 1946 Hesse was awarded the Nobel Prize, though poor health prevented him from attending the award ceremony in Sweden. Hesse died in his sleep in the early morning of August 9, 1962.

SOME INSPIRATIONS BEHIND HESSE'S WORK

Much of Hermann Hesse's work can be traced to his own experiences. Hesse often drew upon personal incidents and wove them into the broader fabric of his writing. For instance, his mental problems, which surfaced after World War I, led him to psychoanalysis. The work of the noted psychoanalyst Carl Jung was an important influence, as Hesse was treated by Jung's protégée, J. B. Lang. Inner conflicts would form the core of many of his later works, including most significantly *Steppenwolf.* Concurrently, Hesse's lifelong interest in Eastern philosophy and religion would surface in *Siddhartha,* which was based loosely on the life of Gautama Buddha. In addition to the Hindu influences, Chinese philosophy would also color Hesse's work. The most overt manifestation of these inspirations was the theme of the search for enlightenment (a search that often draws the protagonist outside of the norms and mores of the contemporary society). Hesse's works also draw upon the earlier work of figures such as Friedrich Nietzche and Fyodor Dostoyevsky, especially in terms of the inner struggles people face in the modern world and the importance of existentialism in Hesse's writings.

The Writer's Work

Hermann Hesse's writings are based on his own life experiences, and his major works are arguably always autobiographical. Most of his novels concern the spiritual and emotional development of a single individual in the course of travel, religious meditation, or personal adventure. A major theme of his works, one that Hesse never fully resolved, is the conflict between personal piety and the desire to experience life to the fullest. Certain aspects of Hesse's own biography made these conflicts central in his life, as well as in the work that grew out of it. The first major factor is his family background, especially the religious dedication and the pietism of his home, which became an essential element in his makeup.

Pietism. Pietism has its roots in the mysticism of Meister Eckhard, Heinrich Suso (or Seuse), Mechthild von Magdeburg, and others in the Middle Ages. This movement had emerged in response to the rationalism of Thomistic philosophy and sought instead the mystical, personal union of the individual soul with God. Of these thinkers Meister Eckhard was of particular influence on Martin Luther's thought, and through Luther, Eckhard's mysticism became a part of Lutheranism and then of Protestantism in general. Pietism emerged out of Lutheranism in the seventeenth century, again in response to the seeming intermediary role of the Church in the relationship between the individual and God but also as a move away from Luther's sharp division between God and man. Pietism was also bound to the concept of the practical Christian life, which included pacifism and service to others as essential to its practice. This movement subsequently exerted a profound influence on intellectual life in Germany in the following centuries, with notables such as Lessing, Bach,

Goethe, Schleiermacher, and others acknowledging their indebtedness. The missionary work of Hesse's father and grandfather provided a foundation for Hesse's search for personal and profound religious experience. The pietistic demand for spiritual purity also fueled Hesse's own pacifism and commitment to help others.

Issues and Conflicts. An important element in Hesse's work is his temperament, which he himself described as inclining him toward a desire for absolutes, an inclination toward skepticism, criticism, and self-criticism. This perfectionism, combined with restlessness and passion for life, drove Hesse to strive for the heights of experience and for its precise expression in language.

As a consequence of his own nature, the protagonists in Hesse's works are obsessed with the resolution of the inner conflict between the passionate, instinctive side of one's character and the rational, positive aspect. The baser side is in conflict with society; the rational side seeks to help and serve others. This is the fundamental theme in Hesse's first novel, *Peter Camenzind,* in which the protagonist ultimately

Hesse, who appears on the left, is seen here with fellow German novelists Thomas Mann (center) and Jakob Wassermann in 1933.

grew older, and by the age of 14, when he was baptized, he had already become a skeptic. He experienced not a loss of faith in his religion but dismay at the rift between religion and the practice of the faith. For Hesse the absolutist, it was essential that one live the Christian life in order to be a Christian.

It was at about this time that Hesse made his momentous decision to become a creative writer. He had weighed the choices of professions, medicine or law or some similar profession, against a career in a trade requiring technical skill. He concluded that he had neither the interest nor ability for either direction and thus decided, on the basis of his own as yet not fully developed writing skills, that creative writing was the only profession for which he was qualified.

Early Success. During his Tübingen years Hesse socialized with students and locals, and he did more than his share of drinking and carousing, frequently with the less-desirable elements of society. At the same time he was still advancing his writing interests; while still working, he managed to publish two works in 1899: *Romantische Lieder (Romantic Songs)* and *Eine Stunde hinter Mitternacht (An Hour behind Midnight)*.

When he succeeded in publishing his first major work, *Peter Camenzind,* in 1904, he had enough money to marry Maria Bernoulli, but the additional financial burden of a wife and growing family obliged the young writer to

succeeds in reconciling these conflicts and in the end finds himself rich in life experience, while serving others in the capacity of innkeeper. This theme carries over into his other novels and reaches its zenith in *Steppenwolf,* where the protagonist experiences the heights and depths of human existence but can conclude only that he will "one day be a better hand at the game."

Adolescence. Hesse notes in one of his autobiographical sketches that he began to lose his respect for the Pietism of his parents as he

produce work at a faster pace, including literary criticism, short works of fiction, and essays. In the following years he wrote *Unterm Rad (Beneath the Wheel)* (1906), *Gertrude* (1909), and, finally, *Rosshalde* (1914).

War and Its Aftermath.

Hesse's involvement in World War I proved a disaster for him. The illness of his son, his wife's worsening mental state, and the reality of the brutal war tore at his always compassionate spirit. These concerns, along with the hostility his pacifism had generated in Germany, drove him to seek psychological counseling. Out of this experience grew an interest in the relatively new field of psychoanalysis, the consequences of which began to appear almost immediately in Hesse's writings. Intense introspection and self-criticism had always been an essential part of Hesse's character, and psychoanalysis only intensified this tendency.

Demian, Hesse's first major publication to come out of this turmoil, was published under the pseudonym Emil Sinclair and purportedly described the youth of its author. Ironically, it was awarded the Fontane Prize for "outstanding first works." Hesse found himself obliged to admit his authorship and return the award. *Demian* was just one of many works appearing under the Emil Sinclair pseudonym during this time in Hesse's life, which is generally referred to as the Sinclair period.

As a consequence of the extensive association of his parents and grandparents with India and other lands of the East, Hesse had inherited a powerful interest in Eastern philosophy, which had been enhanced during his journey to India in 1911. His publication of *Siddhartha* in 1922 was the direct result of this interest. He views Indian thought, however, through the eyes of a Westerner, in his case, a Westerner of deep pietistic conviction. Hesse's own life experiences, which included overindulgence in the sensual pleasures, also find their way into this novel.

Of all his novels, *Steppenwolf* certainly reflects most profoundly the events of Hesse's private life. Written after Hesse's difficult separation from his first wife and divorce from his second wife, the political chaos in Germany, and his plunge into alcohol, drugs,

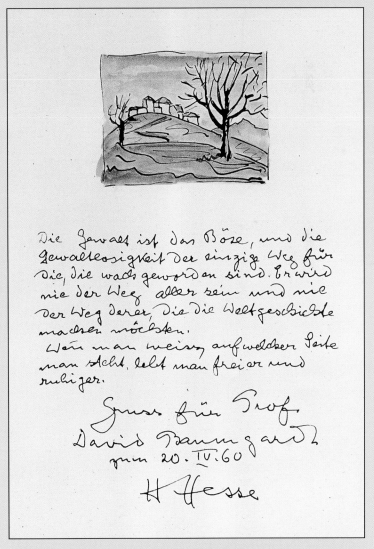

This letter, in which Hesse comments on the forces of good and evil, was written in 1960. Hesse remarks that nonviolence is the only way for the mature individual. He comments on the quieter, freer life one can lead once one knows which side he or she is on. The watercolor is also Hesse's creation.

Both of these photographs, taken 14 years apart by Hesse's son Martin, capture the writer's love of the outdoors. The above, taken in 1937, reveals the pensive, creative side of Hesse as he paints, while the other, snapped in 1951, unveils his delight in relaxation.

and sexual adventure—as well as renewed sessions with a psychoanalyst—*Steppenwolf* explores Hesse's struggle to find resolution between his passionate temperament and his deep religious instincts in this frenzied world. The stylistic approach that Hesse used in this work did not begin with the perspective of the moralist or the classicist, as had been the case in so many of his previous works. Instead, it is an immoralist perspective, the dissonance of which initiates the exploits of its protagonist, Harry Haller, whose initials,

H. H., certainly point to the author as the source of the conflict. Fiction, magic, and fairy tale make up the stuff of the *Steppenwolf* adventure, which, in keeping with its theme of chaos and rejection of moral values, is fragmented. The end of this novel does not bring its protagonist into equilibrium with the chaotic contemporary world but gives him only the hope of faring better on his next attempt.

The interest this work aroused in the following decades reflects the extent to which it

LONG FICTION

1904 Peter Camenzind (English translation, 1969)
1906 Unterm Rad (Beneath the wheel)
1909 Gertrud (Gertrude)
1914 Rosshalde
1919 Demian (Published under the pseudonym Emil Sinclair)
1922 Siddharta (Siddhartha)
1927 Steppenwolf
1930 Narziss und Goldmund (Narcissus and Goldmund)
1943 Das Glasperlenspiel (The glass bead game; also titled Magister Ludi)

SHORT FICTION

1915 Knulp: Three Tales from the Life of Knulp
1914 If the War Goes On: Reflections on War and Politics
1920 Klingsors letzter Sommer (Klingsor's last summer)
1925 Piktors Verwandlungen (Piktor's metamorphosis)
1928 Krisis. Ein Stück Tagebuch (Crisis pages from a diary)
1932 Die Morgenlandfahrt. Erzählung (The journey to the East)

POETRY

1899 Romantische Lieder (Romantic songs)
1902 Gedichte (Poems)
1951 Unterwegs. Gedichte (Wandering: notes and sketches)

Hermann

NARCISSUS AND GOLDMUND

HESSE

---

elicited universal empathy with this personal torment and the inability to come to terms with the confusion evoked by the overwhelming presence of the modern world.

The Glass Bead Game in 1943 marked the close of Hesse's writing career so far as longer creative works were concerned. His eyesight, which had always been poor, was by now failing, and increasingly poor health made his work all but impossible. The Nobel Prize in 1946 provided a recognition of his life's work and was the fitting climax to a long and productive career.

The autobiographical character of Hesse's writings and the focus on internal conflict make them ill designed for drama. Theater requires dialogue, that is, conflict and resolution between individuals that can be represented on the stage. Internal conflict, however, precludes any such staging because it takes place within the individual. For this reason almost none of Hesse's works have appeared on the screen, and the few that have were poorly received by the public.

BIBLIOGRAPHY

Boulby, Mark. *Hermann Hesse: His Mind and Art.* Ithaca, NY: Cornell University Press, 1967.

Casebeer, Edwin F. *Hermann Hesse.* New York: Warner, 1972.

Freedman, Ralph. *Hermann Hesse: Pilgrim of Crisis. A Biography.* 1st ed. New York: Pantheon, 1978.

Helt, Richard C. *A Poet or Nothing at All: The Tübingen and Basel Years of Hermann Hesse.* Providence: Berghahn Books, 1996.

Marrer-Tising, Carlee. *The Reception of Hermann Hesse by the Youth in the United States.* Bern and Frankfurt am Main: Lang, 1982.

Mileck, Joseph *Hermann Hesse and His Critics: The Criticism and Bibliography of Half a Century.* Chapel Hill: University of North Carolina Press, 1958.

Richards, David G. *The Hero's Quest for the Self: An Archetypal Approach to Hesse's "Demian" and Other Novels.* Lanham, MD: University Press of America, 1987.

Rose, Ernst. *Faith from the Abyss: Hermann Hesse's Way from Romanticism to Modernity.* New York: New York University Press, 1965.

Ziolkowski, Theodore. *The Novels of Hermann Hesse: A Study in Theme and Structure.* Princeton, NJ: Princeton University Press, 1965.

Reader's Guide to Major Works

PETER CAMENZIND

> **Genre:** Novel
> **Subgenre:** Bildungsroman
> **Published:** Berlin, 1904
> **Time period:** Early twentieth century
> **Setting:** Switzerland

Themes and Issues. Hesse has often been compared with his contemporary Thomas Mann, with whom he conducted an extended correspondence. Mann concerned himself with the discord between the artist and society: the artist as the outsider, the one who does not belong. Hesse, however, sees this discord not as socially rooted but as the dichotomy between the creative spirit and the practical, the ancient division between the imagination and the application of knowledge of the world. Hesse describes himself, not as one who rejects society, but as one who prefers to live aside from it. Like Hesse himself, the protagonists in his major works are fiercely independent; they are lone seekers after their own identity.

Peter Camenzind was Hesse's first major literary success. Following the death of his mother, Hesse's protagonist goes from his home in a mountain village into the wider world. Amid new temptations, the naive young man matures in spirit and develops as an artist. Hesse says in one of his biographical essays that much of *Peter Camenzind* and also of *Demian* is based on incidents from his own youth, but he does not

Viewed panoramically from the blossoming alpine meadow, the formidable backdrop of rolling hills and steep mountains in John McWirter's painting *An Alpine Meadow* symbolizes the peaks and valleys of Peter's life in Hesse's first novel *Peter Camenzind.*

specify which events they might be. Clearly, Peter's and Demian's quarrels with their parents and their misbehavior in school draw on the author's youth.

The Plot. Peter lives with his mother and father in a small village in the Swiss Alps. Rising early one morning, he finds his mother dying in her bed. He remains quietly at her bedside through the hours as death comes. This first experience with death and dying begins his journey into the reality of human existence. As a boy in school, Peter is bright enough, and his teachers recognize his abilities, though he is clearly not the most intelligent boy in his classes. He is also unruly and an annoyance to his teachers and to other students as well. As soon as he is old enough, he leaves his village to discover the world beyond. This departure marks the beginning of his journey as he learns bit by bit about life, about death and dying, and about himself.

His first friend, Richard, recognizes Peter's creative talents in writing and singing, including yodeling, and encourages him to make use of his skills. Peter's early success comes when Richard gets one of his stories published. Peter's skills as storyteller and clever conversationalist become a passport into the more elevated social circles as well as the taverns of the less-elevated classes. Peter travels with his friend to Italy, where they thrill to sights that they have only heard of before. Peter is profoundly impressed by the beauty of the art and equally taken by the beauty of nature around him. The travelers return to Switzerland, and Richard goes off to Germany, where he dies in a drowning accident. Peter again experiences the death of someone near to him. He attends the funeral and, back in Switzerland, drowns his sorrow in drink. Emerging from his depression, he meets the woman who will become his deepest love, Elizabeth. During one of their countryside walks, she reminds him that he is unlike other men; he is a poet and, as a poet, sees the natural world differently, imbuing it with love. Peter realizes, however, that he has failed to imbue people with that same love.

Peter meets a cripple named Boppi, whom he at first finds repugnant, but reminding himself of his obligation to care for others, he takes Boppi to live with him and eventually comes to love him as a brother. Boppi, too, soon dies, and Peter returns home to his father. The two begin to frequent the local tavern, where Peter and his father share in drinking. Peter has now returned to the place of his youth and becomes a part of the village, like all the others, but now as one who has experienced life.

Analysis. This is Hesse's first major work, and though it is possibly the least significant of all his novels, it does provide a theme that remains central to all his later writings. Unlike many of the writers of the twentieth century, Hesse defines the poet here not as one alienated from society or as one with superior wisdom to be revered and heeded by the world. Rather, he recognizes that the poet sees the world differently and can share his or her vision, help others, and even entertain. Peter Camenzind sees life, sees death and dying, sees all levels of society and assimilates all of what he sees into himself. In the end Peter can return to his small alpine village as a part of the community, but as one who has experienced life.

SOURCES FOR FURTHER STUDY

Boulby, Mark. "Peter Camenzind." In *Hermann Hesse,* edited by Mark Boulby, Ithaca, NY: Cornell University Press, 1967, pp. 1–38.

Roloff, Michael, trans. *Peter Camenzind.* New York: Farrar, Straus and Giroux, 1969.

Werner, Alfred. "Hermann Hesse." *South Atlantic Quarterly* 52, no. 3 (July 1953): 384–390.

SIDDHARTHA

Genre: Novel
Subgenre: Bildungsroman
Published: Berlin, 1922
Time Period: Around 500 B.C.E.
Setting: India at the time of the Buddha

Themes and Issues. Hesse's next major work following *Peter Camenzind* was *Demian,* which,

Hesse's 1922 coming-of-age novel, *Siddhartha*, explores the title character's quest for insight and understanding. Siddhartha, who eventually breaks away from the more socially accepted mode of civilization, finds peace and spirituality in living his life on the river.

much like *Camenzind* before it, follows the process of growth and maturation of its protagonist. With *Siddhartha* Hesse now introduces into his fiction his years of study of India and the Far East. Its protagonist, Siddhartha, is a seeker after spiritual peace. (*Siddhartha* is a name from the Sanskrit *siddha,* "accom-plished," and *artha,* "goal"; thus, "one who has accomplished his goal," an epithet of the Buddha.)

The Plot. Siddhartha is the son of a wealthy Brahmin. He is handsome, intelligent, and beloved of all, and his father expects him to become a great learned man, perhaps a priest. Siddhartha, however, is not content with his life because he has not found inner peace, which he seeks to achieve through meditation and the observation of religious ritual. He stubbornly insists on going forth to live a life of personal sacrifice with the Samanas. He persuades his father to allow him this favor and sets out with his bosom friend Govinda to join the Samanas. After three years of this life and having learned all that he can from his fellow disciples, he leaves to follow Gotama (the Buddha), hoping to find the teaching that will bring him the answers to his search. After hearing Gotama, whom he very much admires, Siddhartha concludes that what he seeks cannot be acquired from teachings or from teachers but must be acquired from contact with the world. Thus, he turns to life among people, but on the way to the city, he encounters the river and the ferryman who will take him across. He spends the night with the ferryman and with the river, which seems to speak to him. As he proceeds to the city, he encounters the beautiful courtesan Kamala, who agrees to teach him the art of love. Kamala also explains to Siddhartha that he must become a wealthy man if he is to court her favor. Introduced to the rich merchant Kamaswami through the intervention of Kamala, Siddhartha becomes an assistant to the merchant and eventually a partner in his business. While continuing his relationship with Kamala, he succeeds in becoming very wealthy, but in the process he gradually succumbs to greed in his desire for money. Realizing that he has lost sight of his quest, he abruptly leaves everything and returns to the dwelling of the ferryman, where in time the experiences of life and the lessons he draws from the river allow him to find his own identity and bring him to his goal of communion with the world. He becomes the ferryman and finally dies in the arms of his old friend Govinda.

Analysis. As in his previous novels, Hesse's protagonist explores the knowledge of the world as it is to be found in reading and in the teachings of wise men as a way of finding himself. In the end Siddhartha finds what he has sought through his experiences in life, that is, in human society and in nature (the river). His final peace of mind comes through finding his place in the world as a ferryman—as one who serves others by carrying them over the river of life and finds solace in this task.

SOURCES FOR FURTHER STUDY

Beerman, Hans. "Hermann Hesse and the Bhagavad-Gita." *Midwest Quarterly* 1 (October 1958): 27–40.

Butler, Colin. "Hermann Hesse's Siddharta." *Monatshefte.* 63, no. 2. (Summer 1971): 117–126.

Rosner, Hilda, trans. *Siddharta.* New York: New Directions, 1957.

STEPPENWOLF

Genre: Novel
Subgenre: Bildungsroman
Published: Berlin, 1927
Time period: Around 1920
Setting: Unspecified location

Themes and Issues. As an aid to recovering from his mental breakdown in 1916, Hesse submitted to psychoanalysis with a Jungian psychiatrist in Lucerne. Out of this experience grew Hesse's preoccupation with the human psyche, the results of which appear first in *Demian* and then later and most extensively in *Steppenwolf.* This is the most complex of all Hesse's writings and the most psychologically profound.

The Plot. The story is divided into two parts; the first, shorter part takes the form of a preface purportedly by the publisher of the manuscript of Harry Haller's notes, which form the second part of the book. The publisher describes to the reader how he came to know Harry Haller, a renter in his aunt's house, and describes Haller in detail, both physically and in behavior and thought (Haller bears a striking resemblance to Hermann Hesse). Haller is middle aged, comes from a good Christian background, and loves music and good books.

He is a collector of books of all sorts and in great quantity. Haller loves Mozart and Beethoven and admires Goethe and Nietzsche, as well as Jean Paul, Novalis, Lessing, Jacobi, and even Dostoyevsky. He drinks, usually moderately but sometimes to excess, and is seen from time to time in the company of beautiful women. The publisher at first suspects that Haller is a foreigner because he seems out of his element in normal society, but as he comes to know Haller better, he begins to see him as a man filled with self-hatred. The author also refers to Haller with increasing frequency as Steppenwolf, a wolf of the steppes, wild and rapacious. Haller one day disappears, never to be seen again, but in his room the publisher finds Haller's records and, because they are of psychological interest, decides to make them public. These records form the second, longer part of the story.

Steppenwolf is characterized as "substituting disorder for reason." In this second part of the story, the reader is presented with Harry Haller's own personal version of his life and, not surprisingly, it is chaotic and seemingly disorganized. The records are subdivided into several segments. The first, titled "For Madmen Only," describes Harry Haller's daily routine, an apparently normal existence underneath which is a life vastly different from that of the people

A wolf, represented here in Carl B. Andreas Ruthart's *A Wolf,* ca. 1650, comes to signify the untamed side of Hesse's alter ego, the character Harry Haller, in his 1927 novel *Steppenwolf.* Ultimately the wolf symbolizes the wilder, more chaotic side of Hesse himself.

around him. Harry Haller expresses an intense dislike for the bourgeois world and its complacency. He is Steppenwolf, the solitary hater of life's conventions. Yet, at the same time, Haller has admiration for this same bourgeois world. He struggles to bring harmony within himself between his chaotic world and the part of him that is a seeker of order.

The subsection titled "The Treatise" defines Steppenwolf. The madness of Steppenwolf comes from substituting disorder for reason. Steppenwolf is like the artist whose life is empty and chaotic and full of despair, out of which a masterpiece is created. The chaotic side can be compared with a wolf's existence, full of pain and suffering; the other side, however, is full of beauty and has a need for the two sides to exist in harmony.

The subsequent sections describe Haller's adventures in the world as Haller sees it in his confused state of mind, and at times it is a drug- induced fantasy world. The events of his life are then shown in a kaleidoscope of fragments. He attends a masked ball where he meets and falls in love with the beautiful Hermine, who is in the guise of a young man (Hermine-Hermann). Although Heller conducts a passionate liaison with Hermine, he shares more spiritual pleasure with Hermine's friends, Maria and Pablo, who is the director of the Magic Theater and a jazz saxophonist.

In the final episode, "Magic Theater," Pablo leads Haller through a series of peep shows, where he sees fragments of his life being portrayed in a pantomime. He also sees Pablo in a passionate embrace with Hermine, and in a jealous rage he kills Hermine. Ready to suffer the punishment for his action—which would be eternal life—he realizes that it has all been illusion, all "magic theater." Pablo now teaches him chess, but this game is played with pieces of his

own being, which are continually rearranged on the board to create ever new personalities.

The novel ends not on a pessimistic note but with muted optimism. In the end Haller has arrived at a better understanding of his world and of himself in it. He is ready to play again but now with the knowledge he has gained and without any assurance of success.

Analysis. In a note at the beginning of the 1961 translation of *Steppenwolf,* Hesse himself remarks that "of all my books *Steppenwolf* is the one that was more often and more violently misunderstood than any other, and frequently it is actually the affirmative and enthusiastic readers, rather than those who rejected the book, who have reacted to it oddly. Partly, but only partly, this may occur so frequently because this book, written when I was fifty years old and dealing, as it does, with the problems of that age, often fell into the hands of very young readers. But among readers of my own age I also repeatedly found some who . . . strangely perceived only half of what I intended. . . .This book, no doubt, tells of griefs and needs: still it is not a book of a man despairing, but of a man believing." Let Hesse's words be the summary of his work.

SOURCES FOR FURTHER STUDY

Flaxman, Seymour. "Der Steppenwolf: Hesse's portrait of the intellectual." *Modern Language Quarterly* 15, no. 4 (December 1954): 349–358.

Fickert, Kurt. "The Development of the Outsider Concept in Hesse's Novels." *Monatshefte* 52, no. 4 (April-May 1960): 171–178.

Hertz, Peter. "*Steppenwolf* as a Bible." *Georgia Review* 25, no. 4 (Winter 1971): 439–449.

Mayer, Hans. *Steppenwolf and Everyman.* Translated and with an introduction by Jack D. Zipes. New York: Crowell, 1971.

Other Works

BENEATH THE WHEEL (1906). *Beneath the Wheel* is one of Hesse's semiautobiographical novels. The book points to the potential dangers of putting too much pressure on young people to succeed academically, especially if the emphasis on academics comes at the cost of normal emotional development.

The central character, Hans Giebenrath, is selected at the age of 14 to compete for entry into a prestigious preparatory school and then go on to study at the seminary (all free of charge). Only 36 youths will be admitted, and Hans faces unrelenting pressure from both his father and his teachers. The emphasis on study prevents him from maturing socially and leaves him isolated from youth his own age. While he passes the entrance exams and makes it through the preparatory school, he has become so mentally and physically drained by the experience that he begins to fall apart emotionally. When his performance at the seminary falters, his father and his teachers put even more pressure on him. He leaves the seminary for a rest, but it is clear that he will never return. Hans dies a broken youth.

DEMIAN (1919). *Demian* was Hesse's breakthrough novel, and it touches upon many of the painful experiences that the writer had as a youth. He wrote the work under the pseudonym Emil Sinclair and presented the book as an autobiography. It contains many of the influences that would characterize his later works, including those drawn from the existential literary tradition and writers such as Nietzche and Dostoyevsky and those drawn from Jung and psychoanalysis.

In the story Sinclair serves as the narrator and main protagonist. The novel traces the young man's growth from childhood to adulthood. On a parallel level the story describes Sinclair's journey from innocence to maturity. Sinclair has a number of mentors and teachers, but the most influential is Max Demian, who helps the young man assert himself and break free of conventional norms of contemporary society. Demian is also directly responsible for Sinclair's final transformation into selfhood, which comes when they both serve during World War I and Sinclair is badly wounded.

NARCISSUS AND GOLDMUND (1930). *Narcissus and Goldmund* is set in medieval Germany. On one level the novel is about two novices, but Hesse uses the characters to explore different paths to self-discovery. In the novel Goldmund wants to live life to the fullest and experience everything. He travels widely and engages in a variety of activities and adventures. Goldmund challenges the conventional morality of the day, and his actions often bring both pleasure and pain to himself and others. Meanwhile his teacher and mentor Narcissus remains within the walls of a monastery as a teacher. Narcissus is presented as a wise and introspective man who is able to learn much about life and himself through prayer and meditation rather than adventure. Although the two characters are polar opposites, they need each other. Goldmund relishes the quiet and routine of Narcissus, while the latter envies Goldmund's zest for life. Ultimately, the relationship between the two allows each to have a greater understanding and appreciation of the world and of himself following their reunion at the end of the book. Hesse uses the story to highlight the differences between the intellectual side of people and their sensual side.

THE JOURNEY TO THE EAST (1932). As with many of Hesse's works, *Journey to the East* is written in an autobiographical style and contains elements of Hesse's own life, even though the work is fiction. The work is one of a number of pieces that were significantly influenced by Eastern philosophy and mysticism, and it would later be read by those who sought to use Hesse's works to renounce Western norms and values and embrace those of the East.

The novel revolves around a group known as the League, which is involved in a journey to the Eastern world. The League is made up of artists, musicians, and writers. The members of the group each have their own private goals during the adventure. For the central character, Hermann, the initial goal is to find the "princess of Arabia." However, problems beset the journey, and eventually Hermann deserts

George Grosz's painting *Street Scene* embodies the social dichotomy that is prevalent in Hesse's fiction. Hesse's characters, though often focused on their own internal conflict and self-analysis, sometimes succeed in reaching a more harmonious existence. Such is the case in Hesse's novel *Narcissus and Goldmund*.

the voyage. Years later he endeavors to write a story about the trip and discovers that many of his assumptions about the journey were false. Ultimately, Hermann rejoins the League after he is granted forgiveness for deserting.

THE GLASS BEAD GAME (1943). *The Glass Bead Game* was Hesse's final and most ambitious work. It took him 12 years to complete. *The Glass Bead Game* combines all of the major elements of Hesse's works, including existentialism, Eastern philosophy and religion, and Jungian psychoanalysis. In the book Hesse endeavored to develop a European version of the ancient Indian social caste system known as the Varnasrama Dharma. The setting for the work is an imaginary place known as Castilia.

Castilia is run by an intellectual elite, and the community focuses on the arts and sciences rather than commerce or war. Central to the community is a cryptic game that strives to bring together different artistic and intellectual pursuits. The main character, Joseph Knecht, becomes Magister Ludi, or Master of the Game. Knecht begins to realize that Castilia is disconnected from the world around it and, hence, from the everyday lives of real people. Knecht strives to bridge the gap between the two worlds but is ultimately unsuccessful.

Resources

Hesse was a prolific letter writer (some 35,000), and he also reviewed some 3,000 works by other authors during his life. Among the major European archives on Hesse is the Swiss National Library at Bern, Switzerland, and the archives of the publishing house Suhrkamp/Insel Verlag in Frankfurt, Germany. The major American collections are housed at the University of Southern California at Santa Barbara.

Books and Writers. This Web site features a biography, bibliography, and links, as well as excerpts from Hesse's writing (http://kirjasto.sci.fi/hhesse.htm).

Hermann-Hesse.com. This site, in English and German, is maintained by the Hesse Museum in Calw. It contains a biography, photographs of Hesse's house, an art gallery with his works, and information about the museum, in addition to links to other resources (http://www.hermann-hesse.com/).

Hermann Hesse Page. Maintained by the University of Southern California at Santa Barbara, this Web site contains an annotated bibliography of the author's works, including plot summaries and analyses, links, and even theses that have been written about Hesse. It also contains the Hermann Hesse Page Journal, an electronic journal about the author. In addition, the Hesse Page operates a listserve (HESSE-L), which facilitates group discussions and readings (http://www.gss.ucsb.edu/projects/hesse/).

Nobel E-Museum. The Nobel Foundation maintains a Web page with information about all of the recipients of its awards. The page on Hesse contains a biography, his acceptance speech, and links to other resources (http://www.nobel.se/literature/laureates/1946/).

Oglethorpe University Museum. This site contains a biography and access to a selection of Hesse's 3,500 watercolor paintings, which can be enlarged and viewed (http://museum.oglethorpe.edu/Hesse.htm).

WILLIAM H. SNYDER

Aldous Huxley

BORN: July 26, 1894, Godalming, Surrey, England
DIED: November 22, 1963, Los Angeles, California
IDENTIFICATION: Twentieth-century English writer best known for his futuristic satire *Brave New World.*

SIGNIFICANCE: Huxley's *Brave New World* is one of the most important novels of the twentieth century. In many parts of the world, its title has become a catchphrase for the misuse of technology to subdue the individual and manufacture an artificial happiness. Although his other works have received far less attention, he was a versatile and subtle writer who raised important issues in both his fiction and nonfiction. A piercing social commentator, Huxley was not afraid to explore the unorthodox or to probe the mysteries of human experience. He was admired as a radical thinker by more than one generation and has proven to be prophetic in what he envisioned for the twentieth century and beyond.

The Writer's Life

On July 26, 1894, Aldous Huxley was born into an illustrious family of scientists, writers, and educators. The third son of Leonard and Julia Huxley, he was the grandson of the biologist Thomas Henry Huxley, a great champion of the theory of evolution. His mother was the niece of the poet and moralist Matthew Arnold and sister of the novelist Mrs. Humphry Ward. She herself was a teacher who founded a private school. Huxley's father was a schoolmaster and then editor of the literary *Cornhill Magazine*.

Childhood. Three traumatic events in Huxley's early life shaped his career. The first was the death of his mother when he was 14. He had been very attached to her and never very close to his father. A few years later he developed a severe eye infection that blinded him for a while and left his vision extremely limited for the rest of his life. The third shock was the suicide of his brother Trevenen.

Huxley made the best of his physical condition, learning braille and joking that at least he could read under the bedcovers. His eye damage prevented him from going into medicine or science, but he did recover enough sight to go from the prestigious preparatory school Eton to Oxford University.

College and War. Shocked by the outbreak of the First World War (1914–1918), Huxley at first wanted to fight but soon lost enthusiasm.

An undated photograph of Eton, the prestigious English preparatory school Huxley attended in the early 1900s. While at Eton Huxley became partially blind from keratitis, an inflammation of the cornea, which dashed his early hope of becoming a physician. After his graduation from Oxford University, Huxley returned to Eton to teach, but he did not enjoy teaching and soon left.

Huxley, far right, is seen here at his son's wedding reception at the New School for Social Research in New York City on April 30, 1950, a few days after the marriage took place. Left to right are the bride's father, Bryan J. Hovde, president of the New School; the bride's mother; the bride, Ellen Hovde Huxley; the groom, Matthew Huxley; and mother of the groom, Maria Nys Huxley.

He was in any case physically disqualified. A bright spot was his inclusion at the house parties at Garsington Manor, where Lady Ottoline Morrell, the famed hostess and patron of a notable circle of artists and intellectuals, entertained many of the prominent intellectuals of the day. It was here that Huxley met his future wife, a Belgian refugee named Maria Nys. While studying for his English literature degree, he wrote poetry and published his first collection, *The Burning Wheel,* in 1916.

Early Writing Career. After graduating with high honors, Huxley tried teaching school and working in the War Office but enjoyed neither. He decided to work in London as a literary journalist and try to launch a writing career. His first novel, *Crome Yellow* (1921), made quite an impression. *Antic Hay* (1923) and *Those Barren Leaves* (1925) confirmed his status as a promising young novelist. He agreed to a publisher's contract that demanded a high rate of production for the rest of his career. This commitment brought security but also the pressure to publish before he was completely satisfied with his work.

He now had a family to support. After marrying Maria Nys in 1919, they were somewhat surprised to find themselves parents by 1920, when their son Matthew was born. Given that Maria was a bisexual and well known as such in her own circles, some were surprised at the match. Nevertheless, it proved to be a long and happy marriage. Maria devoted herself to her husband's care. She was his social guide, his chauffeur, his secretary, and very important, someone who read to him daily so that he could keep in touch with ideas despite his poor eyesight.

The Huxleys lived in Italy and southern France for a time, primarily because the cost of living was lower and the climate better than in London. They also went on a world tour in 1925 and visited Central America in 1933.

HIGHLIGHTS IN HUXLEY'S LIFE

1894	Aldous Leonard Huxley is born on July 26 in Godalming, Surrey, England.
1908	Mother dies of cancer.
1910	Huxley is almost blinded by eye infection while at Eton.
1913	Eyesight improves. Huxley enters Balliol College, Oxford.
1914	Brother Trev commits suicide.
1915	Huxley meets prominent intellectuals at Garsington Manor; also meets future wife, Maria Nys.
1916	Graduates with a first-class honors degree in English literature; publishes first poetry collection, *The Burning Wheel.*
1917	Works in the War Office; teaches at Eton.
1919	Marries Maria Nys; works in London as a literary journalist.
1920	Son, Matthew, is born.
1921	Huxley publishes first novel, *Crome Yellow.*
1923	Lives in Italy.
1925	Sets out on a world tour.
1926	Begins friendship with D. H. Lawrence.
1928	Literary reputation is established with *Point Counter Point.*
1929	Huxley begins friendship with Gerald Heard.
1930	Lives in France.
1932	Publishes *Brave New World.*
1933	Visits Mexico and Central America.
1935	Becomes active in English pacifist movement.
1936	Publishes the conversion novel, *Eyeless in Gaza.*
1937	Accompanies Gerald Heard to the United States and settles in southern California; begins to write screenplays for Hollywood; becomes increasingly interested in Eastern mysticism.
1945	Compiles *The Perennial Philosophy.*
1953	Experiments with mescaline for the first time.
1954	Publishes *The Doors of Perception,* which describes his psychedelic experience.
1955	Death of his wife, Maria.
1956	Huxley marries Laura Archera.
1959	Receives the Award Merit Medal of the American Academy of Arts and Letters.
1960	Is nominated for the Nobel Prize in literature.
1961	House fire destroys Huxley's manuscripts.
1962	Huxley is elected a Companion of Literature of the British Royal Society of Literature.
1963	Dies in California on November 22; memorial service is held in London on December 17.

Huxley befriended D. H. Lawrence in the mid-1920s, nursed him through his last illness, and then edited his letters in 1932. With the publication of *Point Counter Point* (1928) and *Brave New World,* (1932) Huxley's reputation neared its peak.

Conversion. In the mid-1930s Huxley joined the pacifist movement and began to lecture for the Peace Pledge Union. He was trying to complete an ambitious novel, *Eyeless in Gaza* (1936), but suffered a writer's block and a bout of depression (a Huxley family trait). Eventually, he emerged with a completed manuscript and a serious interest in mysticism. His pacifist stance made him unpopular with some, but he retained it for the rest of his life.

Move to America. In 1937 Huxley took his message to America with his fellow pacifist Gerald Heard. After their lecture tour he decided to stay. Like other European writers, Huxley settled in Los Angeles in the hope of writing for Hollywood. He also thought the climate would improve his health and vision. The Hollywood career did not quite materialize, though Huxley was involved in some productions, most notably, adaptations of Jane Austen's *Pride and Prejudice* (1940) and Charlotte Brontë's *Jane Eyre* (1944). Some in Britain criticized him for remaining in America once war broke out in Europe, even though there was no chance he could have served.

Mysticism. Now a resident in California, Huxley became increasingly interested in Eastern mysticism, in particular a form of Hinduism known as Vedantism. However, he was never a formal disciple of any guru and disliked organized religion and dogma of all

Huxley with his second wife, Laura, in the latter half of the 1950s.

kinds. Another long-term interest was in alternative approaches to healing and training the body, mind, and spirit. Some of these techniques are now considered orthodox, but others turned out to be passing fads. Huxley claimed that alternative treatments improved his eyesight, but those who knew him were not convinced. His circle of friends by now included film stars such as Greta Garbo and Charlie Chaplin, the composer Igor Stravinsky, and the astronomer Edwin Hubble.

Psychedelics. In the mid-1950s Huxley experimented with psychedelic drugs such as mescaline and LSD. He did so legally and, initially, under medical supervision, in the hope that these substances would expand his con-

Aldous Huxley grew up in a family known for its high intellectual achievement, and he was no exception. He combined the Huxleys' fascination with science with the Arnolds' quest for spiritual values. His grandfather coined the term *agnostic,* and agnosticism was Huxley's religious attitude until he found a nondogmatic form of spiritual belief. His longtime friend Gerald Heard was instrumental in sustaining this conversion.

Huxley's social position gave him entry into the upper-class intellectual circles that were the setting for much of his writing. Though he spent nearly thirty years in America, he remained in speech and manner an English gentleman.

Renowned English biologist Thomas Henry (T. H.) Huxley (1825–1895), Aldous Huxley's paternal grandfather, seen here around 1880, was a great supporter of Charles Darwin's theory of evolution. While attending one of many Darwinian debates in 1860, Bishop Samuel Wilberforce made the grave error of voicing an offensive inquiry about T. H. Huxley's simian ancestry, whereupon T. H. Huxley turned to his neighbor and replied, "The Lord hath delivered him into mine hands." When it was T. H. Huxley's turn to reply, he did so with overwhelming effect, stating that if he had to choose between an ape for a grandfather and a man who chooses to introduce "ridicule into a grave scientific discussion, I unhesitatingly affirm my preference for the ape." Like his grandfather, Aldous Huxley was deeply interested in both science and theology and was dedicated to having a better understanding of where, and if, the two converge and diverge.

sciousness and allow him to achieve a mystical awareness. He used them as occasional aids, but it is not clear that Huxley ever enjoyed a full-blown mystical experience. He argued that these substances altered brain chemistry less crudely than traditional practices such as fasting and flagellation, but he seemed unaware of the potential for widespread abuse. His own self-evolution seemed to be progressing. Friends had always noted his gentle and kind nature, but in later years some thought he became also more at peace with himself, even serene.

Later Years. Huxley's lowest point was reached when Maria died of cancer in 1955. The account of how he eased her passage into death is very touching. He remarried in 1956,

to Laura Archera, an Italian musician and psychotherapist. In 1960 he was diagnosed with cancer of the tongue but declined surgery. A house fire in 1961 destroyed all but a few of his belongings. Huxley apparently took it philosophically as a great spiritual clearance. In his last years he was a visiting professor at the University of California at Santa Barbara, MIT, Berkeley, and the Menninger Foundation. He was nominated for the Nobel Prize in 1960 and elected a Companion of Literature in Britain in 1962 (an honor restricted to just ten living writers). His nationality remained British because his pacifist beliefs barred him from becoming an American citizen. He died in 1963 on November 22. A memorial service was held in London a month later.

The Writer's Work

Aldous Huxley was a versatile and prolific writer who produced novels, short stories, poems, essays, travelogues, biographies, anthologies, screenplays, and plays. He is known primarily as a novelist but was most comfortable as an essayist.

There are two distinct reasons to read Huxley: for his witty and sophisticated account of his own era and milieu, particularly upper-class English intellectual life, and for the way he raised the great, eternal questions—why are we here? and how should we live? Huxley served as an intellectual who did more than entertain. He made the novel a forum for ideas, or as one reviewer remarked, he equipped it with a brain.

Recognition came early. Huxley burst onto the scene as a shocking and original commentator and gained an international reputation by the time he turned thirty. He then underwent a profound and gradual transformation from a restless satirist to a religious thinker. Cynical satires gave way to more earnest, moralistic novels involving a search for spiritual fulfill-

Ideas seem to flow effortlessly from Huxley, the quintessential idea man, while being interviewed on November 6, 1948, during his first visit to England in twelve years.

ment. At this point he became less highly regarded as a fiction writer, although he was still being read. Critics may have disliked his ideas and his interest in mysticism as much as his imperfect literary craftsmanship. This dislike led to the neglect of some accomplished later work, particularly the novels *Time Must Have a Stop* (1944) and *Island* (1962).

Novel of Ideas. Huxley did not feel suited to or sufficiently interested in telling stories for their own sake. He was not concerned with

LONG FICTION

1921 Crome Yellow
1923 Antic Hay
1925 Those Barren Leaves
1928 Point Counter Point
1932 Brave New World
1936 Eyeless in Gaza
1939 After Many a Summer Dies the Swan
1944 Time Must Have a Stop
1948 Ape and Essence
1955 The Genius and the Goddess
1962 Island
1998 Jacob's Hands (with Christopher Isherwood; written in the 1940s)

SHORT FICTION

1920 Limbo
1922 Mortal Coils
1924 Young Archimedes
1926 After the Fireworks
1930 Brief Candles
1938 The Gioconda Smile: A Story

NONFICTION

1923 On the Margin
1925 Along the Road
1925 Jesting Pilate
1926 Essays New and Old
1926 Proper Studies
1929 Do What You Will
1930 Vulgarity in Literature
1931 Music at Night
1932 Texts and Pretexts

1934 Beyond the Mexique Bay
1936 The Olive Tree
1937 Ends and Means
1940 Words and Their Meanings
1941 Grey Eminence
1942 The Art of Seeing
1945 The Perennial Philosophy
1946 Science, Liberty and Peace
1950 Themes and Variations
1952 The Devils of Loudun
1954 The Doors of Perception
1956 Heaven and Hell
1956 Tomorrow and Tomorrow and Tomorrow
1958 Brave New World Revisited
1960 On Art and Artists
1963 Literature and Science
1969 Letters of Aldous Huxley (edited by Grover Smith)
1977 Moksha: Writings on Psychedelics and the Visionary Experience (1931–1963) (edited by Michael Horowitz and Cynthia Palmer)
1978 The Human Situation (edited by Piero Ferrucci)
1992 Huxley and God (edited by Jacqueline Hazard Bridgeman)
1994 Between the Wars: Essays and Letters (edited by David Bradshaw)

POETRY

1916 The Burning Wheel
1917 Jonah
1918 The Defeat of Youth
1920 Leda

PLAYS

1931 The World of Light
2000 Now More Than Ever (written 1932–1933)

SCREENPLAYS

1940 Pride and Prejudice
1943 Madame Curie (uncredited)
1944 Jane Eyre
1948 A Woman's Vengeance
1951 Alice in Wonderland (uncredited)

Point Counter Point

ALDOUS HUXLEY
introduction by Nicholas Mosley

"A powerful and vitriolic indictment of the intellectual world."—*New York Times*

perfecting the craft of the novel. Instead he wanted to dramatize ideas, to show the effect of ideas on characters and their world. This overriding desire to convey thoughts and beliefs accounts for many of his strengths and weaknesses.

An impressive breadth of reference is characteristic of both his fiction and nonfiction. Huxley had a keen amateur interest in numerous fields and particularly appreciated the bizarre and the extraordinary. What is most distinctive, however, is his interest in science. There are more references to scientific matters in Huxley's fiction than in any other contemporary's work. It was the writer's duty, he believed, to bridge the two "cultures" of literature and science and bring the human significance of modern science to a wide audience.

Issues in Huxley's Works. Throughout his career, the social problems that most engaged Huxley's attention were the proper use of science and technology, ecology, eugenics, religion, overpopulation, war, and nationalism. His thinking was ahead of its time in many of these areas. When first published, his books were often controversial for their frank portrayal of sex as a basic impulse divorced from love. Later he was again controversial for

his advocacy of pacifism, drugs, and mysticism.

Accommodating both religion and science was another perennial theme. Huxley was searching for a credible theology for the intelligent person after science had undercut traditional beliefs and war had shown Europe to be morally bankrupt. Many of his scientific refer-

Huxley, characteristically harsh and unfair to himself in his portrayals of unattractive autobiographical characters, is seen here covering his eye in 1957.

ences are used to puncture human pretensions, but there is also a serious attempt to see if the less materialistic nature of modern physics can be reconciled with spirituality. Huxley identified a new modesty in the scientists' claims to understanding nature and thought it left room for other approaches to the larger questions.

At the center of Huxley's thought is the relation of the mind to the body. In much of his writing, the flesh is seen as degrading to the mind and spirit. It brings pain, suffering, and all kinds of humiliation. Huxley looked for ways to bring mind and body into harmony and believed both religion and science confirmed their ultimate interconnection. This belief explains his interest in certain types of mysticism, mind-body training, drugs, and parapsychology. In some instances he embraced dubious techniques, but in others he showed great foresight.

People in Huxley's Fiction.

Huxley did not create in-depth portraits. There is generally just enough action to put people into contact with each other and generate some dialogue, but characters rarely develop, except for those who experience sudden conversions. Many are viewed as repulsive or grotesque specimens, and though several of the more unattractive characters bear some resemblance to their author, it has often been remarked how much nicer Huxley was than his partly autobiographical creations.

Usually Huxley's characters are divided within themselves and separated from each other. Common types recur. There are depressed and self-destructive loners, usually male, who are usually the victims of heartless manipulators of various kinds. Then there are less malicious but selfish scientists and artists. Almost everyone is detached and egotistic. In later novels Huxley attempted to portray wholly good characters: celibate commentators who provide higher insight but who are removed from and have little effect on the action. The challenge, which Huxley rarely met, was to make them credible or even likable as characters.

Huxley's Legacy.

Huxley will be remembered first as the author of *Brave New World* and then for his example of giving play to ideas in fiction. Many works are still worth reading for their attention to issues that are only now beginning to be addressed, such as ecology, population control, nonverbal education, and holistic medicine. His ability to think about the alternative and the unorthodox made Huxley influential in more than one rising generation. He was forever interested in freeing the mind and expanding consciousness, as is apparent in his demolition of Victorian attitudes in the early novels or later his experimentation with chemical means for mind expansion in the 1950s. In that sense, he never grew old.

BIBLIOGRAPHY

Bedford, Sybille. *Aldous Huxley: A Biography.* New York: Knopf/Harper and Row, 1974.

Bowering, Peter. *Aldous Huxley: A Study of the Major Novels.* New York: Oxford University Press, 1968.

Deery, June. *Aldous Huxley and the Mysticism of Science.* New York: St. Martin's Press, 1996.

Dunaway, David King. *Aldous Huxley Recollected: An Oral History.* New York: Carroll and Graf Publishers, 1995.

—-. *Huxley in Hollywood.* New York: Harper and Row, 1989.

Ferns, C. S. *Aldous Huxley: Novelist.* London: Athlone Press, 1980.

Firchow, Peter. *Aldous Huxley, Satirist and Novelist.* Minneapolis: University of Minnesota Press, 1972.

Keuhn, Robert, ed. *Aldous Huxley.* Englewood Cliffs, NJ: Prentice-Hall, 1974.

May, Keith. *Aldous Huxley.* New York: Barnes and Noble, 1972.

Meckier, Jerome. *Aldous Huxley: Satire and Structure.* London: Chatto and Windus, 1969.

—-, ed. *Critical Essays on Aldous Huxley.* New York: G. K. Hall, 1996.

Thody, Philip. *Aldous Huxley: A Biographical Introduction.* London: Studio Vista, 1973.

POINT COUNTER POINT

Genre: Novel
Published: London and New York, 1928
Time period: 1920s
Setting: London

Themes and Issues. The most substantial of Huxley's social satires, *Point Counter Point* depicts an upper-class jungle of self-absorbed individuals competing for attention and gratification. It captures the confusion and emptiness of an era that saw the overthrow of traditional religious and moral values. The issue Huxley raises is how to live a fully human and balanced life. In particular, he wonders how humans can cope with suffering and death. At this point mysticism is not a clear solution.

The Plot. Instead of one main plot, Huxley intertwines several subplots that offer variations on common themes. Much of the time is spent in great homes, restaurants, and occasionally even a scientific laboratory. A few of the more prominent characters are unfulfilled writers. The first is Walter Bidlake, a naive young man who has tired of his current mistress and is now lusting after a spoiled heiress, Lucy Tantamount. The second, Philip Quarles, is a middle-aged novelist whose emotional distance almost drives his wife into another's arms until her suitor is murdered. In contrast to this largely unhappy cast, there is a mutually supportive couple, the Rampions, who together reconcile class differences and provide an

example of a balanced and harmonious life. For other characters there are affairs, betrayals, boredom, disillusionment, and sadistic behavior in the bedroom and beyond.

Analysis. Regarded by many as his most accomplished novel, this work is perhaps where Huxley took the conventions of the novel most

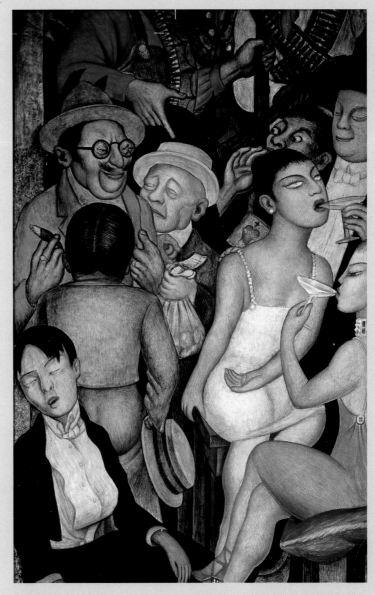

Diego Rivera's *Orgy—Night of the Rich (La Orgia)* reflects an era void of religious and moral values and captures the egotistical, gratification-searching qualities of the characters in Huxley's 1928 novel, *Point Counter Point.*

seriously. The most unusual feature is the use of *counterpoint,* a term Huxley borrowed from music, to describe the juxtaposition of different narrative lines throughout the novel or of different points of view within a scene. He uses it to represent increasingly specialized and compartmented views of reality, none of which adds up to a meaningful whole. As the story jumps rapidly from scene to scene, the reader realizes that the characters are unhappy because they are trapped in their own limited perspectives. They travel forever along parallel tracks without being able to expand their perspective or learn from one another.

The only positive philosophy is voiced by Rampion, who is clearly modeled after D. H. Lawrence. Rampion advocates a balance between mind and body, reason and emotion, but his impact is minimal. The others remain lopsided and addicted: the dry intellectuals, the self-destructive loners, and the bored seductresses. A few are naive; others are hypocritical. Almost all are completely egotistic.

SOURCES FOR FURTHER STUDY

Bowering, Peter. *Aldous Huxley: A Study of the Major Novels.* New York: Oxford University Press, 1969.

Firchow, Peter. *Aldous Huxley, Satirist and Novelist.* Minneapolis: University of Minnesota Press, 1972.

May, Keith. *Aldous Huxley.* New York: Barnes and Noble, 1972.

Meckier, Jerome. *Aldous Huxley: Satire and Structure.* London: Chatto and Windus, 1969.

Roston, Murray. "The Technique of Counterpoint." In *Critical Essays on Aldous Huxley,* edited by Jerome Meckier. New York: G. K. Hall, 1996.

BRAVE NEW WORLD

Genre: Novel
Subgenre: Dystopian fiction
Published: London and New York, 1932
Time period: Twenty-sixth century (632 "after Ford")
Setting: London

Themes and Issues. This is a classic utopian text that has only gained in relevance since it was first written. In *Brave New World* Huxley foresees, among other things, test tube babies, cloning, prozac, the contraceptive pill, the influence of advertising and mass media, vocational education, and state control of scientific research. It is an early depiction of a society dependent on mass consumption and a lack of political involvement. Essentially, the new world applies the principle of mass production to people. Huxley saw the danger in what he called technological idolatry, a belief that technological advance automatically means human progress. In a foreword to the novel written 15 years later, he concluded that humankind was closer to his futuristic nightmare than anyone could have imagined when he first wrote it.

The Plot. The setting is London, now part of a World State 600 years into the future. Introductory chapters reveal how both the society and its citizens are carefully designed. Everyone is grown in bottles and genetically engineered before birth. After birth an individual is psychologically conditioned to fit into a predestined social function through the use of techniques developed by the Russian physiologist Ivan Pavlov and the use of hypnopaedia (sleep teaching). The result is five castes of standardized human beings, from Alpha managers to semimoronic Epsilons. Thanks to conditioning, each person thinks his or her position and makeup is ideal. The lower castes are cloned in large numbers, families no longer exist, and ten benign World Controllers oversee everything and make sure the system remains stable. Stability is secured through daily use of the euphoric drug soma, frequent and promiscuous sex, and a careful balance of work and mass entertainment. A secular religion structured on the ideas of Henry Ford, the inventor of mass production, also compels orthodox behavior. Its rituals include state-mandated orgies. The only exception to this new world order is the existence of some reservations, where, because of poor climate and lack of natural resources, the people are left in primitive squalor.

The action focuses initially on Bernard, a peevish Alpha Plus misfit. After dating Lenina

The limp, robotlike body in Susanne Schuenke's 1989 painting *The Sleeper* communicates the sense of defeat felt by the inhabitants of a futuristic world populated by mass-produced human beings in Huxley's 1932 groundbreaking masterpiece of utopian fiction, *Brave New World*.

for a while, he brings her to a New Mexico reservation. There, among the filth and disease, they encounter Linda and her son, John, who Bernard suspects are the former lover and illegitimate son of his boss. He is permitted to return with them to London, where John "the Savage" is indeed revealed to be the son of the Director of Hatcheries and Conditioning, much to the Director's embarrassment. This public humiliation allows Bernard to escape punishment for his unorthodox attitudes and even become popular while he escorts John around London. Bernard becomes arrogant. He neglects his only friend, Helmholtz, a very talented Alpha Plus writer who is too creative for his assigned role. Lenina is attracted to John, but though the attraction is mutual, John

spurns her advances because he acts under different, more puritanical rules. Meanwhile, Linda overdoses on soma and soon dies.

Pained by his mother's death and disgusted by the World State's reduction of humanity, John tries to incite a riot. At this point he is brought to the Western World Controller Mustapha Mond, along with Bernard and Helmholtz. Mond calmly reveals to them the reasons for his society's attitude to science, art, history, and religion. He acknowledges that in return for comfort, health, and contentment, society has sacrificed freedom, individualism, heroism, passion, dignity, and joy. Once happiness is guaranteed, states Mond, there is no need for God or religion. He and John debate the relative merits of "civilized" society and the reservation, but Huxley does not indicate which of the two extremes is the more absurd.

After meeting with Mond, Bernard and Helmholtz are sent to the Falkland Islands to be with other discontented Alpha intellectuals. Bernard greets the news with a cowardly collapse, and Helmholtz, with quiet dignity. Forced to remain in England, John camps out on the edge of civilization. However, fixated on his lust for Lenina and guilt over his mother's death, he engages in sadomasochistic behavior, which soon attracts attention. When Lenina appears on the scene, he gets involved in a frenzied orgy. The next day, in a bleak ending to the novel, he commits suicide. In a later foreword to the novel, Huxley remarks that, if he had written the novel later, he would have offered some choice between John's primitivism and the World State.

Analysis. *Brave New World* is Huxley's best-known work and will probably ensure his international reputation for some time to come. The title comes from William Shakespeare's *The Tempest,* where a naive Miranda marvels on first seeing other humans, "O wonder! How many goodly creatures are there here! How beauteous mankind is! O brave new world, that has such people in it." As John gets to know the World State and its flaws, the phrase becomes increasingly ironic.

The visitor who uncovers the flaws of the new society is an established utopian convention. More generally, the didactic and satiric nature of utopian literature suited Huxley well. In this novel he presents his often ingenious ideas economically and comically. A lecture tour at once immerses the reader in the new world and outlines its main features. In the third chapter several interlocking conversations provide a succinct and amusing account of its history and principles. Pervasive slogans and jingles reveal more standardized beliefs.

The focus of both the society and the narrative is on the social system rather than the individual. So the thinness of the characters becomes a deliberate point rather than a fail-

ing on the writer's part. Huxley's two-dimensional characters work here because they demonstrate how shallow this society has made its citizens.

SOURCES FOR FURTHER STUDY

Baker, Robert S. *"Brave New World": History, Science, and Dystopia.* Twayne's Masterwork Studies, no. 39. Boston: Twayne, 1990.

Bowering, Peter. *Aldous Huxley: A Study of the Major Novels.* New York: Oxford University Press, 1969.

Deery, June. "Technology and Gender in Aldous Huxley's Alternative (?) Worlds." In *Critical Essays on Aldous Huxley,* edited by Jerome Meckier. New York: G. K. Hall, 1996.

De Koster, Katie. *Readings on "Brave New World."* San Diego, CA: Greenhaven Press, 1999.

Firchow, Peter. *The End of Utopia: A Study of Aldous Huxley's "Brave New World."* Lewisburg, PA: Bucknell University Press, 1984.

May, Keith. *Aldous Huxley.* New York: Barnes and Noble, 1972.

Meckier, Jerome. *Aldous Huxley: Satire and Structure.* London: Chatto and Windus, 1969.

ISLAND

Genre: Novel
Subgenre: Utopian fiction
Published: London and New York, 1962
Time period: 1960s
Setting: Island in Southeast Asia

Themes and Issues. *Island* is an antidote to *Brave New World;* it transforms many of the latter's negatives into positive means to fulfillment. Now different forms of psychedelic drugs, conditioning, eugenics, and sex are seen as beneficial. The emphasis is on limited production and consumption, individual development, and ecological balance. While *Brave New World* represented the triumph of technology over religion, here technology is kept in its place. Priority is given to the art of living over other arts or sciences. To aid each person's development, this society has made remarkable innovations in education, health care, and family life, some of which are less radical now than when Huxley first wrote about them.

The Plot. After a sailing accident, Will Farnaby, a journalist, finds himself on the island of Pala, an ideal society ordinarily closed to visitors. Once rescued, he is permitted to stay and get to know the ingenious synthesis of Eastern and Western traditions begun over a hundred years earlier by a Scottish doctor and a native Buddhist ruler. Will, however, is on a secret mission to help his employer open up Pala for oil exploration. This assignment brings him into contact with two disaffected insiders: the next monarch, Murugan, and his egotistic mother, a former princess of neighboring Rendang. While Will negotiates with them, he comes to admire Palanese society and begins to regret his role in endangering its future. He finally disengages from the other conspirators and reveals the plan, perhaps risking his job. His only comfort is that some takeover was about to happen anyway. Meanwhile he is granted a spiritual experience with the help of a psychedelic substance called moksha. The novel ends with the tanks of Rendang coming in to crush this fragile experiment and exploit the land's natural resources.

Analysis. Huxley's last major work is best appreciated if approached not as a regular novel but as a partially dramatized essay. The visitor, Will, seems to be impressed by everything he sees, so there is little conflict until the last moment. Some concrete enactments are useful, as when Will witnesses schoolchildren being trained to literally stamp out anger or when he has lunch with an extended family and learns how to "chew grace." As in all of his later fiction, however, Huxley faces the difficulty of creating credible virtuous characters, a difficulty he does not entirely surmount.

Yet the novel is also warm and even touching at times. The portrayal of a peaceful death scene reflects the author's coming to terms with the death of his mother and his wife and with his own impending end; it creates a real emotional charge. Elsewhere, Huxley knew that the high ratio of ideas might cost him some readers, but he was still disappointed that more people did not take his ideas to heart. More than a novel, *Island* was a sincere attempt to offer practical solutions on how to live. It may be that it has yet to find its fullest audience.

SOURCES FOR FURTHER STUDY

Bowering, Peter. *Aldous Huxley: A Study of the Major Novels.* New York: Oxford University Press, 1969.

Ferns, C. S. *Aldous Huxley: Novelist.* London: Athlone Press, 1980.

May, Keith. *Aldous Huxley.* New York: Barnes and Noble, 1972.

Meckier, Jerome. *Aldous Huxley: Satire and Structure.* London: Chatto and Windus, 1969.

Watt, Donald J. "Vision and Symbol in Aldous Huxley's *Island.*" In *Aldous Huxley,* edited by Robert E. Kuehn. Englewood Cliffs, NJ: Prentice-Hall, 1974.

Other Works

CROME YELLOW (1921). Huxley's first novel is more charming, high-spirited, and sunny than his later works. A weekend house party brings together a mixture of eccentric aristocrats, artists, and intellectuals for some witty conversation. The story drifts along idly with amusing digressions into the curious and the grotesque.

EYELESS IN GAZA (1936). Some regard *Eyeless in Gaza* as Huxley's greatest novel, while others view it as fatally flawed and unnecessarily difficult to read. Most agree that it is a serious spiritual biography containing more psychological depth than is seen elsewhere in Huxley's fiction. The story of the central character, Anthony Beavis, is told through radical shifts back and forth in time. After suffering childhood pain and loss, he became an irresponsible and egotistic adult, but later, after meeting Dr. Miller, Anthony adopts a mystical perspective and becomes an active member of

The individuals in the center panel of Otto Dix's 1928 *Grosstadt* (Big Town) mirror the high-spirited eccentricity of the characters at the party in Huxley's first novel, *Crome Yellow.* The novel started to build Huxley's reputation as a skilled satiric novelist. As the story unfolds, the grotesque is revealed, as it is on close examination of *Grosstadt,* which appears at the Galerie der Stadt Stuttgart in Stuttgart, Germany.

the pacifist movement. He finds that spiritual self-awareness brings real freedom, as distinguished from simply doing whatever one feels like in a meaningless context.

AFTER MANY A SUMMER DIES THE SWAN

(1939). Huxley's first novel set in America is a biting satire of William Randolph Hearst, the newspaper tycoon and later subject of the classic film *Citizen Kane* (1941). The story is a strongly plotted farce. The Hearst figure, Jo Stoyte, is a vulgar millionaire whose massive art collection is no consolation for his overwhelming fear of death. In desperation he employs a Dr. Obispo to find a way to prolong his life. The scientist discovers that the secret to long life is to eat carp entrails. Obispo also finds time to seduce the tycoon's young mistress, Virginia. Stoyte, in a jealous rage, mistakenly shoots an idealistic young research assistant, Pete. Meanwhile, a wise neighbor, Mr. Propter, preaches mysticism and performs good works, but he has little impact on the others. The ending is grotesque and pessimistic. The manipulative villain triumphs, and an innocent is murdered. As for the secret to longevity, eating carp eventually turns humans into subhuman apes.

TIME MUST HAVE A STOP (1944). Some regard *Time Must Have a Stop* as Huxley's most accomplished novel. Certainly Huxley himself thought it was his best attempt to integrate fiction and ideas. In it he gives full expression to the pleasure of the artistic and the sensual—everything from the composition of poetry to the enjoyment of a fine meal—even as he cautions that true joy lies on a higher plane. The topic is again spiritual conversion, but this time it is depicted with warmth and compassion, perhaps because Huxley is now secure in his own beliefs. A strong, interlocking plot clearly illustrates moral cause and effect, but

there is compassion for those who succumb to temptation. A unique feature is the very experimental description of an after-death experience, which puzzled many contemporary readers but becomes much clearer when understood in the light of Huxley's model, *The Tibetan Book of the Dead.*

The story involves a self-absorbed young poet, Sebastian, who enjoys a visit to his cosmopolitan uncle in Italy. However, soon after Sebastian's arrival, Uncle Eustace dies. In an effort to obtain a promised dinner jacket, Sebastian lands others in trouble, most gravely his cousin Bruno, one of Huxley's most sympathetic mystic figures. Huxley states in an epilogue that Sebastian encountered Bruno ten years later, nursed him during his final illness, and was inspired by Bruno's example to begin his own spiritual education.

THE DOORS OF PERCEPTION (1954). *The Doors of Perception* is a brief, firsthand account

Huxley is seen here speaking at a conference on "A Pharmacological Approach to the Study of the Mind" at the University of California at San Francisco on January 26, 1959. At the conference Huxley stated his prediction that drugs will be the means by which future dictators will enslave the earth. Although Huxley experimented with drugs himself, he never intended *The Doors of Perception,* his 1954 firsthand account of his experience on mescaline, to be an open-door invitation for others to try psychedelic drugs.

of Huxley's first psychedelic experience. Under medical supervision Huxley took a small dose of mescaline and enjoyed a stunningly vivid perception of the world around him. He describes at one point seeing what Adam must have seen on the morning of his creation, "the miracle, moment by moment, of naked existence." It was a tremendous release from Huxley's usual near blindness. As well as clarity of vision came a sense that everything has intrinsic significance once one removes the normal filters and, in the poet William Blake's words, opens the doors of perception.

Huxley's stance is intellectual, even scientific, but the drug clearly allowed him to experience what up until then he had only read about. He notes, however, that the experience is so engrossing that there is no motivation to do any good in the world. He recognizes this as a serious problem. He also acknowledges that the mescaline experience can be hellish and does not guarantee a mystical experience, even though some thought he was making this claim. He certainly did not intend his sober experiment to promote a recreational use of psychedelic drugs, though such a state of affairs may have been the result. This book gained him the admiration of Timothy Leary and others in the 1960s counterculture. The book's title also inspired Jim Morrison and his legendary rock band to name themselves the Doors.

Resources

Although most of Huxley's manuscripts were lost in a fire in 1961, some manuscripts and typescripts can be found at the Humanities Research Center, Austin, Texas; at the University of California, Los Angeles; and at the New York Public Library. Other organizations of interest to students of Aldous Huxley include the following:

The Centre for Aldous Huxley Studies. This center is the home of the international Aldous Huxley Society, based in Germany. Founded in 1998, this organization provides information on activities and research concerning the author. It sponsors an annual conference and promotes the academic study of Huxley's works—in particular, critical editions, commentaries, and interpretations. The society's *Aldous Huxley Annual* publishes essays on the life, times, and interests of Huxley and his circle (www.anglistik. uni-muenster.de/Huxley).

Gravity of Light. This 1996 documentary by the Canadian filmmaker Oliver Hockenhull is subjective and impressionistic. Unusual visual effects, personal essays, and archival footage are used to reexamine Huxley's life and ideas. Topics include technology, drugs, and religion.

Huxley Hotlinks. This Web site offers links to on-line information about Huxley and his works, with an emphasis on psychedelics and *Brave New World* (http://www.huxley.net/hotlinks.htm).

Soma Web. This is a fairly comprehensive site with links to material on Huxley and, most prominently, *Brave New World*. It includes criticism, audio clips, a detailed bibliography, and on-line texts of Huxley's works (http://somaweb.org/).

JUNE E. DEERY

Eugène Ionesco

BORN: November 26, 1909, Slatina, Romania

DIED: March 28, 1994, Paris, France

IDENTIFICATION: Twentieth-century Romanian-French playwright best known for being an originator of absurdist theater.

SIGNIFICANCE: Ionesco's plays ushered in the radical movement in theater referred to as theater of the absurd. Departing from accepted stage conventions, he used language, objects, and actors in playful and innovative ways. He managed to imbue profound subject matter, such as death and the anguish of life, with great vitality and vivid images. His first play, *The Bald Soprano,* premiered in 1950, when he was 40 years old, and he continued to create a body of work into his eighties. He has inspired a generation of playwrights, including such illustrious figures as Tom Stoppard and Harold Pinter. His plays are internationally acclaimed, and *Rhinocéros* (1959) is considered an absurdist classic.

Childhood. On November 26, 1909, in the city of Slatina, which lies along the Olt River in southern Romania, Eugen Ionescu (later adapted to Eugène Ionesco) was born to a Romanian father and a French mother.

Thérèse Ipcar (Icard), Ionesco's mother, was the daughter of a French engineer who had settled in Romania. Ionesco's father, Eugen, was studying to be a lawyer and gave his first son his own name. A year or so after Ionesco's birth his sister, Marilina (Regine), was born and then a year later, a brother, Mircea, who died of meningitis at the age of 18 months. When Ionesco was very young, the family moved to Paris, where he first had exposure to puppet shows, which began to fire his interest in theater.

Family Influences. As a small child Ionesco's consciousness was molded by the unstable nature of his parents' marriage and, later, his father's absence from their life. His parents separated while in Paris, and in 1916 Ionesco's father abandoned the family while he presumably went to fight in World War I. Thérèse was forced to work in a factory to sustain the family during this period.

After the war the family assumed Eugen had been killed in battle. Later Thérèse's investigations revealed that her husband had not even served in the war. In 1917 he had returned to Romania, arranged a divorce from Thérèse on falsified grounds so that he could remarry, and became a chief of police in Bucharest. In addition, he had used his position to get official custody of the children. Eugène and his sister moved to Bucharest in 1922 to live with Eugène and his new wife, Lola.

At this time Eugène began learning the Romanian language and attended the Sfântul Sava school. Lola, the stepmother, did not like the children and soon drove Eugène's sister out of the house. Eventually the situation at his father's house became intolerable for Eugène, and at the age of 17, he moved out to live on his own.

College Years. Eugène and his father continued to have a volatile relationship throughout his years in school, though his father did give him some monetary support. In 1928 he earned his baccalaureate at the secondary

Ionesco with his wife of almost sixty years, Rodica Burileanu, in the late 1970s or early 1980s.

school in Craiova. In that same year he first began to have his writing published in *Bilete de papagal* (Parrot notes), which appeared daily. He published his first article in the *Zodiac* in 1930. At this time he met his future wife, Rodica Burileanu, a student of philosophy and law. He went on to obtain a degree in French from the University of Bucharest.

While at the university he began writing poetry, articles, and political and dramatic criticism. When he wrote *Nu (No!)* (1934), which was a series of articles and diary notes, he made his first major venture into existentialism. This assault on traditional Romanian literature caused an outrage in literary circles and was a sample of the authoritarian rebelliousness Ionesco would exhibit in his life and writing.

The year 1936 proved to be an eventful year for Ionesco, as he married Rodica Burileanu in July, and three months later, his beloved mother, Thérèse, died of a stroke. During this time Ionesco worked as a French teacher, taught seminars, supervised a section of the *Facla* review, and wrote for various publications. In 1938 he took the opportunity to move to Paris on a Romanian scholarship to write a thesis (it was never finished).

War Years. At the beginning of World War II, Ionesco returned to Romania and worked as a French teacher in Bucharest. He hated the pro-Nazi political climate in Romania, and in his diaries from this period, it is apparent how alone Ionesco felt in his beliefs. It is also here that he first uses the word *rhinoceros* in relation to those who were converting to the political ideology. (Later, Ionesco used this image as the central idea of his most popular play.) He tried desperately to leave Romania during this period. Finally, with the help of friends, he and his wife were able to return to France.

Life was difficult financially for the couple in France. Ionesco and his wife had a daughter, Marie-France, born on August 26, 1944, and they moved to Paris in 1945.

Sometime after 1936—the exact date is in question—Ionesco had a last meeting with his

FILMS BASED ON IONESCO'S PLAYS

1962	*Seven Deadly Sins* (one segment)
1966	*The Bald Soprano*
1968	*The Lesson*
1973	*Rhinoceros*
1975	*The New Tenant*
1987	*Eugène Ionesco: Voices Silences*
2001	*I Return to the House* (based on *Exit the King*)

father. They had a violent political disagreement, and Ionesco said, "It is better to be on the side of the Jews than to be a stupid idiot. My regards to you, sir," and then left. Those were his last words to his father. Ionesco later expressed some remorse over how this meeting ended. His father died 12 years after his mother, the same year he began work on his first play.

The Playwright Emerges. In 1948 Ionesco began work on what became a groundbreaking play, *The Bald Soprano*. The first performance occurred on May 11, 1950. Except for the accolades of a few of the French intelligentsia, however, the play was received poorly.

Despite the disappointing response to *The Bald Soprano,* Ionesco continued to vigorously write and produce plays with existential views. He produced *The Lesson* in 1951; *The Chairs, The Motor Show,* and *Victims of Duty* in 1953; *Amédée* in 1954; and *Jack, or the Submission* in 1955. All these plays were pub-

This photograph, taken on February 9, 1994, was the last one taken of Ionesco. He died almost seven weeks later, on March 28, 1994.

HIGHLIGHTS IN IONESCO'S LIFE

1909	Eugène Ionescu is born in Slatina, Romania.
1910–1912	Moves with family to Paris.
1922	Returns to Romania.
1928	Earns baccalaureate degree; first poetry is published in *Bilete de papagal*.
1930	First article appears in the *Zodiac* review.
1931	Ionesco writes *Elegies for Tiny Beings*.
1933	Earns graduate degree in French.
1936	Marries Rodica Burileano.
1938	Returns to France.
1939	Returns to Romania.
1942	Escapes to France.
1945	Earns doctorate.
1948	Gains French citizenship; father dies.
1950	Ionesco produces *The Bald Soprano* at Théâtre des Noctambules under the director Nicolas Bataille.
1951	Produces *The Lesson.*
1954	Publishes first four plays in France.
1959	Publishes *Rhinoceros;* is a participant in International Theatre Institute Congress in Helsinki.
1962	Publishes *Notes and Counter Notes* and *Exit the King.*
1968	Publishes *Present Past, Past Present: A Personal Memoir.*
1969	Receives medal of Monaco and Great National Theatre Prize.
1971	Gains admission to Académie française.
1987	Théâtre de la Huchette celebrates 30th anniversary with Ionesco and his wife present.
1989	Ionesco receives Molière Prize.
1994	Dies in Paris, France, on March 28.

lished for the first time in 1954. By the mid-1950s he had established his reputation as a playwright, thanks in part to the strong support he received from the renowned French playwright Jean Anouilh and the novelist Raymond Queneau. Then in 1957 came the true turning point—the tiny Théâtre de la Huchette staged a double bill of *The Lesson* and *The Bald Soprano*. The acclaim this production received gained Ionesco recognition as a major force in the theater, and he was now on his way to becoming an internationally known and respected playwright.

In addition to those works already mentioned, Ionesco continued to write plays until late in life. Ionesco also wrote about the theater in *Notes and Counter Notes* (1962), *Present Past, Past Present: A Personal Memoir* (1968), and the novel *The Hermit* (1974).

Ionesco's most popular works are those written between 1950 and 1965. His attack on fascism and the Nazi movement, *Rhinoceros*, is probably the play for which he is best known. Zero Mostel starred in the Broadway production in 1961; it was a huge success, ran for 241 performances, and assured Ionesco's status as a world-renowned playwright. A planned Broadway staging of *Journeys among the Dead* (1980), his last play, was canceled before opening.

Later Years. After receiving numerous awards and worldwide recognition, the high point of Ionesco's fame came in 1971, when the Romanian-born playwright was honored with membership in the prestigious Académie française, the French Academy.

Ionesco was a member of the Comité international des écrivains pour la liberté (International Committee of Writers for Liberty), which works on behalf of human rights and for artistic independence. He stopped writing in his later years and spent his time painting and exhibiting his works. Ionesco died in Paris on March 28, 1994, of undisclosed causes.

PLAYS

1952 The Bald Soprano
1954 The Lesson
1954 The Chairs
1954 Jack, or the Submission
1954 The Future Is in Eggs
1954 Victims of Duty
1954 Amédée
1955 The Leader
1958 The New Tenant
1958 The Killer
1958 The Master
1958 Maid to Marry
1958 Improvisation
1958 The Picture
1959 Rhinoceros
1959 Scene with Four
1963 Pedestrian of the Air
1963 Exit the King
1963 Salutations
1963 Anger
1964 Hunger and Thirst

1966 The Gap
1970 The Killing Game
1972 Macbett
1973 Hell of a Mess!
1974 Plays of Massacre
1975 Man with Suitcases
1975 Stories for Children
1980 Journeys among the Dead

MEMOIRS

1962 Notes and Counter Notes
1968 Fragments of a Journal
1968 Present Past, Past Present: A Personal Memoir

NOVEL

1974 The Hermit

OPERA LIBRETTO

1988 Maximilien Kolbe

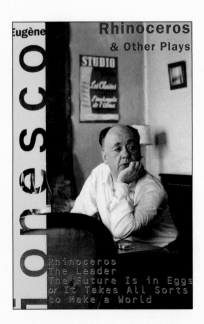

Eugène Ionesco primarily wrote plays. However, he also wrote poetry, philosophical and political essays, and children's stories. He was a member of the innovative group of avant-garde artists that emerged in the wake of the pessimism and despair that swept Europe after World War II. He is best known for breaking with the conventions of traditional theater and creating bold new approaches to the stage.

Ionesco felt that *his* world made more sense than the "real" world. In *Notes and Counter Notes* he says, "I could even go so far as to say that to me it is the world that seems irrational, that is growing irrational and baffles my understanding." Fueled by the philosophies of existentialism and absurdism, Ionesco espoused the view that there were no absolutes and so the whole of existence was meaningless.

He wanted theater to be larger than life, a place of power, images, and passion. He wanted his plays to stand on their own, absurd or not; they never try to convey a "message," as did the standard French "boulevard" theater. The rebel artist in him did away with the conventions of plot and character development in favor of absurd dialogue and broad theatricality. He imaginatively intertwined tragedy and comedy. Ionesco was almost 40 years old, however, before this rebelliousness manifested itself in playwriting, though it had long been present in his nature.

The Young Writer Emerges. The nonconformist in Ionesco first surfaced when he was a young man in Romania. His free-spirited beliefs were in stark contrast to the oppressive

Ionesco (far right) with his wife, Rodica, at the Théâtre de la Huchette in Paris, where *The Lesson* and *The Bald Soprano* appeared together in 1957. This production brought Ionesco instant acclaim and, finally, recognition as a serious playwright.

Ionesco's theatrical imagination found its first expression when he was a small child. His mother would take him to the Punch and Judy puppet shows at the Luxembourg Gardens in Paris. In *Notes and Counter Notes* he says he was there, all day long, "open-mouthed, watching those puppets talking, moving and cudgeling each other. It was the very image of the world that appeared to me, strange and improbable but truer than true." Thirty-five years later, the form of truth that Ionesco began to bring to the world in his body of plays was a reflection of this theatrical, cartoonlike, and enthralling world.

It is impossible to talk about Ionesco's work without addressing existentialism. Yet existentialism is a varied doctrine that is difficult to define. Espoused by philosophers such as Søren Kierkegaard, it alleges that the individual is alone in an alien world, has his or her own personal truth, and makes decisions based on that truth. Compared with the age-old view that truth and moral values are unitary, this was a revolutionary outlook. In *The Killer, Rhinoceros, Pedestrian of the Air,* and *Exit the King,* Ionesco's character Berenger is the ideal existentialist hero: a man in an unceasing quest for his own individualism.

One of the primary sources of Ionesco's inspiration was the process of growing old and dying. When he was four, his mother explained to him, in the context of a burial procession, that people died because they grew old. When he asked her if everyone grows old and dies, she answered yes. Ionesco said, "Then I started to scream and cry. I must have cried for hours." A preoccupation with death and dying haunted Ionesco all his life and appears in almost all of his plays.

Children watch a Churchill puppet hit a Hitler puppet over the head in this wartime Punch and Judy puppet show in Surrey, England, in 1941. Punch and Judy shows were Ionesco's first exposure to theatrics.

Nazi ideology, and they put him in conflict with his father, who was a member of the Nazi-controlled Iron Guard.

Ionesco and his father were on opposite sides of the spectrum in their approach to political ideologies. Ionesco believed that it was essential to oppose established authority, whereas his father staunchly believed in following the position of the state. This conflict with his father was a key factor in forming Ionesco's life as a writer.

Beginning in 1928, when he had his first poetry published in the daily *Bilete de papagal,* Ionesco continued to write articles for *Today,* *Flower of Fire, Literary Romania,* the antifascist magazine *Critica,* and *Zodiac.* In 1931 his first volume of poetry, *Elegies for Tiny Creatures,* came out, and the controversial volume of essays called *No!* appeared in 1934. After going to France on a scholarship in 1938, he found himself back in Romania at the beginning of World War II.

The Discovery of a New Kind of Theater.
During the war Ionesco and his wife managed to escape from Romania to France. In 1948, while studying the English language, Ionesco inadvertently began work on what would be his

first play, *The Bald Soprano.* While copying the simplistic dialogue of the characters into his phrasebook, he realized the power of repetitive, everyday language. This realization inspired him to bring the robotlike characters Mr. and Mrs. Smith to life. He turned their trite conversations into illogical discussions. He used the rhythm of the action to shape the speech so that the language became like another character—a meaningless one. All at once, in this simple, one-act play, Ionesco had devised a new way to look at the world and created a whole new terrain in the world of the theater.

Development of the Playwright.

Ionesco's intense period of writing plays lasted almost 40 years. The second play he produced, *The Lesson,* has a homicidal professor who uses words and rhetoric as a means of wielding power over a student. Once again, language is the main culprit.

The Chairs, performed in 1952, was a turning point for two reasons. It was the first play to introduce the surrealistic idea that objects, as much as language, represent obstacles in human life. In addition *The Chairs* brought a new reality to his characters—the old man and woman were more alive emotionally, and the audience could identify with them. Six years passed before this human reality appeared in his characters again.

The soulful character of Berenger, said to be Ionesco's alter ego, first appears in *The Killer,* produced and published in 1958. Much like Ionesco, Berenger is a rebel and classic nonconformist who opposes the forces of the universe; in this case he stands up to a ruthless killer. In Berenger, Ionesco had finally created a human, down-to-earth character with whom audiences could identify—the true everyman.

Berenger appears again in 1959 in Ionesco's most popular play, *Rhinoceros.* Berenger is the only character that does not succumb to becoming a rhinoceros as he stands up to the pressures of society. Reaffirming Ionesco's own staunch resistance to fascism, this obviously anti-Nazi play is an attack against mass hysteria.

Berenger appears in two more of Ionesco's plays. In *Pedestrian in the Air* and *Exit the King,* both produced in 1962, Berenger is again the man who stands up to the system. In *Exit the King,* considered Ionesco's most traditional play, King Berenger is facing the ultimate opponent—his own death. The king yields in the end. Here Ionesco used his theatrical techniques to perfection to allow the audience to actually experience what death might feel like.

In his later plays Ionesco continued to employ absurd language, objects, and mechanized behavior but added a more conventional plot structure. His early work depicted symbolic, cartoonlike characters, such as the Smiths and Martins in *The Bald Soprano,* but later he created characters with a human soul who struggled against insurmountable odds. Thus, the audience could identify both with Berenger's anguish and with his courage in *Rhinoceros* and *Exit the King.*

Ionesco's primary theme concerns how the individual defines his own truth in this alien world and then fights for his beliefs. However, his plays also address the absurdity of life, the inability to communicate, the dehumanization of society, and the terrifying and inevitable nature of death. Another recurring theme, best expressed in *Amédée,* his first full-length play, published in 1953, is the difficulty of living together as man and wife. Ionesco continued to write plays into his ninth decade. He also wrote the libretto for an opera, *Maximilien Kolbe,* and a novel titled *The Hermit.*

BIBLIOGRAPHY

Bonnefoy, Claude. *Conversations with Eugène Ionesco.* New York: Holt, Rinehart and Winston, 1971.

Coe, Richard N. *Ionesco.* New York: Barnes and Noble, 1965.

Jacobsen, Josephine, and William R. Mueller. *Ionesco and Genet: Playwrights of Silence.* New York: Hill and Wang, 1968.

Lamont, Rosette C., ed. *Ionesco: A Collection of Critical Essays.* Englewood Cliffs, NJ: Prentice Hall, 1973.

Pronko, Leonard C. *Eugène Ionesco.* New York: Columbia University Press, 1965.

Wager, Walter, ed. *The Playwrights Speak.* New York: Delacorte Press, 1967.

THE BALD SOPRANO

Genre: One-act play

Subgenre: Absurdist play

Published: France, 1952; first production, 1950, Paris

Time period: Indeterminate

Setting: A middle-class English home

Themes and Issues. While studying the English language at the age of 39, Ionesco had the idea for his first play, *The Bald Soprano.* Ionesco took his inspiration from the home-spun truths revealed in the language lessons in his workbook. He created a simple plot around the conversation and dialogue of middle-class English householders. By using emotionless characters and broadly exaggerated language, he created a new style of theater. Though not critically well received, it launched a new genre, the theater of the absurd.

Both the title and content of *The Bald Soprano* happened almost by accident. Ionesco intended the first drafts of the play to be a writing exercise, but his friends were so amused and de-

Actors Mary Grace Canfield and Gary Moffat appeared in the Sullivan Street Playhouse production of Ionesco's *The Bald Soprano* in New York City in June 1958. The four cigarettes in Moffat's hand point to the mindlessness of Ionesco's characters and Ionesco's trademark style of absurdity run amok.

lighted with his readings that they encouraged him to put the draft in production. In 1950 a group of young actors under the director Nicolas Bataille gave the first performance of the play. Bataille did not like the original title. During one of the first rehearsals, an actor made a mistake when saying the words "blond soprano"; "bald soprano" came out. In an interview with Rosette Lamont, Ionesco said, "We all laughed, and the mistake became the title of the play. Of course, we also changed the reference within the play. This made it even wilder—which is exactly what I was aiming for."

The Plot. The play opens with a typical middle-class English couple sitting in armchairs in their living room. Mr. Smith is smoking a pipe and reading a newspaper, while Mrs. Smith is knitting.

Mrs. Smith begins the dialogue with a speech: "There, it's nine o'clock. We've drunk the soup, and eaten the fish and chips, and the English salad. The children have drunk English water. We've eaten well this evening. That's because we live in the suburbs of London and because our name is Smith." Mr. Smith clucks his tongue at various intervals, while Mrs. Smith, talking about a series of unimportant everyday details, mixes logic and nonsense. She chatters on about English beer, potatoes fried in fat, soup, Romanian yogurt, and a doctor who had his liver operated on even though he was not ill. This discussion ends with the clock striking seven times, then three times followed by silence.

The topic of conversation now changes to the Bobby Watsons. As the conversation develops the audience learns that there is an entire family of Bobby Watsons. The husband and the wife, as well as the aunts, uncles, cousins, sons, and daughters, all have the same name. At this point Mary, the maid, announces that the Smiths' guests, Mr. and Mrs. Martin, are at the door. The Smiths exit at this point in order to change their clothes.

The dialogue between Mr. and Mrs. Martin begins with Mr. Martin saying, "Excuse me, madam, but it seems to me, unless I'm mis-

taken, that I've met you somewhere before." They continue questioning each other and make a series of discoveries—that they live on the same street, in the same building and in the same flat. Eventually their discussion leads them to the fact that they each have a daughter, both of whom look the same and have the same name. The discovery of how much they have in common leads Mr. Martin to realize that he and Mrs. Martin are indeed man and wife. After this realization, they fall asleep in the same chair. The clock strikes 29 times.

Mr. and Mrs. Smith return in the same clothes. With the clock striking at odd intervals, the scenes now grow more disjointed, and the words carry less and less significance. The doorbell rings three times; there is no one there until, finally, on the fourth ring the Fire Chief appears. The following conversation takes us further into Ionesco's madcap world:

MR. SMITH [to the Fire Chief]: And what were you doing at the door?
FIRE CHIEF: Nothing. I was just standing there. I was thinking of many things.
MR. MARTIN [to the Fire Chief]: But the third time—it was not you who rang?
FIRE CHIEF: Yes, it was I.
MR. SMITH: But when the door was opened, nobody was in sight.
FIRE CHIEF: That was because I had hidden myself—as a joke.
MRS. SMITH: Don't make jokes, Mr. Fire Chief. This business is too sad.

As there are no fires to put out, the Fire Chief begins to tell nonsensical stories. Here the dialogue begins to break down further, now making even less sense. The clock continues striking more often, and the volume rises as the characters become more agitated.

At this point Mary recites a poem as the Smiths push her offstage. The Fire Chief exits. The four remaining characters spew meaningless dialogue in a final scene that grows into completely infuriated screaming into each other's ears. The stage lights go out, and only the voices are heard giving confused messages.

Finally, even the words stop. Ionesco's directions now are, "Again, the lights come on. Mr. and Mrs. Martin are seated like the Smiths at the beginning of the play. The play begins again with the Martins, who say exactly the same lines as the Smiths in the first scene."

Analysis. *The Bald Soprano*, at first reading, appears to be a critique of English middle-class everyday life. Yet Ionesco knew nothing of the English, and the setting of the play stemmed only from the fact that he was studying conversational English at the time. Ionesco, using the Smiths and Martins as dehumanized representatives of a new world, targets the empty chatter of a cliché-ridden life.

Ionesco creates a caricature of language in *The Bald Soprano;* by doing so, he is able to display the broad stereotypes that people fit into. There is little regard for the basic dramatic elements of plot or character development. Ionesco originally thought the play was a farcical tragedy about language and the emptiness of our lives. However, people found it funny. In juxtaposing the elements of tragedy and comedy, Ionesco created a world at once terrifying and absurdly funny. This strange interweaving, along with the play's open stance against the typical theater offering of the period, led Ionesco to subtitle *The Bald Soprano* an "antiplay."

SOURCES FOR FURTHER STUDY

Block, Haskell M., and Robert G. Shedd. *Masters of Modern Drama.* New York: Random House, 1962.

Edney, David. "The Family and Society in the Plays of Ionesco." *Modern Drama* 28, no. 3 (1985): 377–399.

Grossvogel, David I. *The Blasphemers: The Theater of Brecht, Ionesco, Beckett, Genet.* Ithaca, NY: Cornell University Press, 1962.

RHINOCEROS

Genre: Play in three acts
Subgenre: Absurdist play
Published: France, 1959; first produced, 1959, Düsseldorf, Germany
Time period: Present
Setting: Midday on a Sunday in summer in a small provincial town

Themes and Issues. Ionesco's rhinoceros is a herd animal, thick skinned and capable of violence. In the play, characters, one by one, give up their individuality and become rhinoceroses. Ionesco draws on his own experience of the rise of Nazism to speak out against totalitarian regimes. In the end only Berenger, the lead character, remains human, as everyone around him submits to the mindless strength of the herd.

The Plot. A sunny, hot Sunday finds Berenger, hung over and in yesterday's clothes, meeting with his friend Jean, who is dapper and cheerful. Jean is severely critical of Berenger's appearance and lack of self-respect. Throughout the play, he admonishes Berenger to "improve himself."

Suddenly there is chaos as a rhinoceros appears in the square. Everyone is amazed, including Jean, the waitress, the grocer and his wife, the café proprietor, the old gentleman, the logician, and the housewife with her cat. Jean remarks how strange it is to see a rhinoceros on the street. Berenger sits unmoved and sulking.

Daisy enters. Berenger has a romantic interest in Daisy, who works in his office. He is embarrassed and shy, as Jean continues to admonish him for his appearance. From across the street it is clear that another rhinoceros is stampeding. The onlookers argue about whether it has one horn or two. They ponder whether it is the same rhinoceros or another one. At this point it is discovered that the rhinoceros trampled the housewife's cat, and as she laments, the others console her.

The beginning of act 2 takes place in Berenger's workplace. Dudard, Botard, and Papillon, coworkers, are arguing with Daisy, as she tells them about seeing the rhinoceros. Berenger says he saw it as well, and Daisy presents a newspaper report about a rhinoceros stamping a cat to death.

Mrs. Boeuf enters and relates how a rhinoceros chased her and at the same time announces that her husband is missing. Looking down from the window, she recognizes her

Actor Zero Mostel, who performed in the 1961 Broadway production of Ionesco's play *Rhinoceros,* skillfully exhibits the facial contortions that are all part of the transformation from human being to rhinoceros, from independent thinker to mindless follower.

husband as the rhinoceros waiting for her below, and she leaves to join him. The other employees, visibly shaken, all decide to go home; they hear news that at least 32 rhinoceroses have been reported.

The next scene takes place in Jean's bedroom, since he is ill and in bed. Berenger has come to apologize to Jean for his manners the day before concerning the rhinoceros. Neither recognizes the other's voice. Berenger notes a bump on Jean's forehead. As they are talking, Berenger watches his friend's skin gradually harden and turn green and his voice turn hoarse. Meanwhile, Jean is in denial about anything happening to him. Berenger explains how Mr. Boeuf turned into a rhinoceros. Jean becomes more agitated and defends rhinoceroses in their discussion, and by the end of the scene, Jean completely transforms into a rhinoceros.

Berenger is quite upset now that Jean is a rhinoceros, as he has always liked and respected Jean. Berenger is quite afraid that he too will be tempted to become a rhinoceros. His coworker Dudard comes to see Berenger at his home and reveals that their boss, Papillon, has turned into a rhinoceros. Daisy enters, and all three talk about how the rhinoceroses are running up and down the streets tearing everything apart. Dudard gradually softens his view toward the rhinoceroses and decides he wants to join them. Then he leaves to become a rhinoceros.

Daisy and Berenger are now the only human beings. They talk about re-creating the human race together, but Daisy weakens. She wants to join the rest, since the rhinoceroses seem happier than she and Berenger. Finally, Daisy leaves to become a rhinoceros.

Now Berenger is the only human being left. He begins to weaken. The desire to become a rhinoceros is overwhelming, but he cannot do it. Berenger refuses to give up, and as the play ends, he says, "I am not capitulating!"

Analysis. *Rhinoceros* is probably Ionesco's best-known play. The first French production was in Paris at the Odéon Theatre, where the great Jean-Louis Barrault directed and played the role of Berenger on January 25, 1960. In April of that same year, the first British production was presented at the Royal Court Theatre in London under the direction of Orson Welles and starred Laurence Olivier as Berenger and Joan Plowright as Daisy. These productions brought Ionesco into the mainstream. Critics found in *Rhinoceros* a way to legitimize Ionesco, who up to then had been a peripheral but interesting avant-garde playwright. The Berenger character had appeared in his earlier plays *The Killer* and *Pedestrian of the Air;* by featuring a character with some history, Ionesco makes *Rhinoceros* all the more palpable despite the still dehumanized figures that inhabit the play.

SOURCES FOR FURTHER STUDY

Guthke, Karl Siegfried. "The Modernity of Tragicomedy." In *Modern Tragicomedy: An Investigation into the Nature of the Genre.* New York: Random House, 1966.

Pronko, Leonard C. *Eugène Ionesco.* New York: Columbia University Press, 1965.

Other Works

THE KILLER (1958). Ionesco introduces his recurring character Berenger in this three-act play. In act 1, the wide-eyed Berenger is praising the Architect of the "radiant and perfect city." He is horrified to find out that the Killer is murdering many people every day. Back at his home in act 2, Berenger accidentally finds evidence of the Killer in his friend Edouard's briefcase, and he decides they must take it to the police. In act 3 Berenger is pulling Edouard along in his efforts to reach the police, but the journey is slow. First, Berenger finds out

Edouard has left behind the briefcase that contains the only proof. Then a political rally and a traffic jam get in the way. Berenger sends Edouard back to get the briefcase. Finally, wandering around, Berenger meets the Killer, who does nothing but chuckle. Berenger does all the talking and finally gives in to the Killer and is defeated.

In this play Berenger fights for pure and idealistic beliefs. He loses, but the important point is that he fights and exhibits very human emotions. When Berenger appears next, in *Rhinoceros*, where he fights society and wins, Ionesco paints it as a lonely victory.

PEDESTRIAN OF THE AIR (1963). Derived from his short story "The Colonel's Photograph,"

Pedestrian of the Air was written in 1962. Berenger reappears in this play. This time Berenger is a playwright who is on a walking tour in England with his wife and daughter. As he walks, he has such a sense of exhilaration that he actually begins to walk on air and fly off into space. He returns in a completely transformed state, however, after having seen a vision of horrible disaster and destruction for all mankind. Although this Berenger's conflict is quite different from the ones the first two Berengers had, in common with them he still refuses to give in to those elements of life he finds inhuman.

EXIT THE KING (1963). Berenger appears for the fourth and final time in the tragicomedy

The confident man in Jonathan Borofsky's painting *Man Walking in the Sky,* painted in the early 1990s, mimics the determination of Berenger in Ionesco's 1963 play *Pedestrian of the Air* as he walks off into the sky, unaware of any danger to come but nonetheless prepared to meet whatever challenge lies before him.

Exit the King, also written in 1962, as the aging King Berenger the First. Ionesco has refined his craft here; there is a depth not seen in his other plays. It is also his most traditional play, with all the characters realistically drawn with emotions of their own.

Exit the King is a dreamlike encounter with emotional and spiritual upheavals in the final hours of a human life. Surrounded by his dwindling consortium, including Queen Marguerite (his first wife), Queen Marie (the second wife), and the Doctor, the King is facing the end of his long life. Coming to terms with his imminent death, he experiences denial, self-pity, anger, reminiscence, and finally ac-ceptance of his mortality. The Doctor paints the stark reality for Berenger when he says, "You will have no breakfast tomorrow morning." The audience is present at the end of Berenger's life not as spectators but as participants in the process of dying.

Berenger and his two wives form a triangle; their relationship ebbs and flows, and a man grasps for life as it trickles away from him. On one level, Berenger as the king represents humankind itself. He has lived for centuries through the golden era of his kingdom, and now the forces of nature are calling him. His surrender will en-sure the return of life, and the kingdom will flourish once again—but not with him.

Resources

There is a vast amount of information about Ionesco available to an interested student.

Bald Soprano (Opera). Martin Kalmanoff composed a one-act opera based on *The Bald Soprano;* a video recording made in 1999. It is available in the collection at Ohio University. More information can be obtained at the Web page provided by the university library (http://alice.library.ohiou.edu/search/t b a l d + s o p r a n o / t b a l d + s o p r a n o / 1 , 1 , 3 , B / frameset &F=tbald+sprano&1,,3).

Documentary Film. *Eugène Ionesco: Voices Silences* (1987), a documentary film by Thierry Zeno, may be found in the film collection in the library at Carnegie Mellon University in Pittsburgh, Pennsylvania. The primary attraction of this one-hour film is that Ionesco himself can be seen giving descriptions of his paintings and interpretations of his plays (http://www.library.cmu.edu/ Services/Video/filmog_artbio.html).

Gale Research Group. This Web site provides information on the Discovering Authors 3.0 CD-ROM (1996), which includes detailed information on Ionesco. (http://www.galegroup.com/pdf/facts/dis-aucd.pdf). An excellent selection of the information from the CD-ROM is available at the Web site of New Kensington, Pennsylvania, Valley High School (http://nkasd.wiu.k12.pa.us/vhs/daion.htm).

Théâtre de la Huchette. Though they are difficult to obtain in any form in North America, the filmmaker Jean Ravel created films of *The Bald Soprano* (1966) and *The Lesson* (1968) with Nicholas Bataille and the Théâtre de la Huchette.

Web Sites. Søren Olsen's Web site provides the most comprehensive information on Eugène Ionesco that can be found almost anywhere (http://www.ionesco.org). The information on Ionesco on Shay Goosens Web page is also excellent (http://www.geocities.com/ Broadway/Stage/1052/ionesco2.htm). Another good source is Edward Einhorn's Ionesco Festival Homepage, 2001 (http://www.untitledtheater.com/).

KATHERINE BACON

James Joyce

BORN: February 2, 1882, Rathgar, Dublin, Ireland
DIED: January 13, 1941, Zurich, Switzerland
IDENTIFICATION: Irish novelist, highly acclaimed for his experimentation with modernist techniques of writing, his erudition, his meticulous realism, and in his last two major novels, his comic outlook on life.

SIGNIFICANCE: Joyce is widely regarded as the greatest writer of the twentieth century. His recognition came slowly, but with his masterpiece, *Ulysses,* critics began to study all of his works more carefully and to recognize his genius. His more approachable fiction—the short stories and *A Portrait of the Artist as a Young Man*—is taught in many high schools, and the later, more difficult *Ulysses,* in many colleges and universities. However, his last work, *Finnegans Wake* (probably the most difficult novel in the English language and the scores of other languages into which it has been translated), still defies any definitive understanding, even for many Joyce experts.

The Writer's Life

James Joyce was born on February 2, 1882, the first surviving child of John Stanislaus Joyce and Mary Jane Murray in a marriage that resulted in three miscarriages, four boys, and six girls. James's father, John Stanislaus, was a flamboyant, hard-drinking man with a quick wit and fine tenor voice. Although the Joyces claimed distant noble lineage going back to their migration to Ireland from Wales in the thirteenth century, the Joyce family's roots for several generations had been in Cork, where they owned a number of properties, all of which were mortgaged away as John tried job after job following his marriage to Mary and the growth of their ever-expanding family. In Joyce's heavily autobiographical novel, *A Portrait of the Artist as a Young Man*, Joyce's fictional surrogate, Stephen Dedalus, tells his friend Cranley that his father was

> . . . a medical student, an oarsman, a tenor, an amateur actor, a shouting politician, a small landlord, a small investor, a drinker, a good fellow, a storyteller, somebody's secretary, something in a distillery, a tax gatherer, a bankrupt and at present a praiser of his own past.

It was a remarkably accurate account of Joyce's own father's life. As John Stanislaus's fortunes declined and his drinking continued unabated, the family fell into ever more dire poverty, and they faced eviction after eviction. The succession of addresses at which they lived marked their social decline, and it was only to get them out that a landlord would give them a sufficient recommendation to rent another house and move on.

Education. Joyce's education began in one of the most prestigious Jesuit boarding schools in Ireland, Clongowes Wood, but his father was forced to remove him when tuition became an insurmountable burden. Joyce spent some time in a lower-class Christian Brothers school (a fact he never mentioned in his fiction) before the former rector of Clongowes got him a scholarship to another Jesuit preparatory school, Belvedere College, in Dublin. Joyce was a brilliant, highly verbal, prizewinning student who on graduation in 1898 entered the Royal University in Dublin. The institution, founded by Cardinal Newman and later known as University College, Dublin, became the major institution in Ireland for Catholic undergraduates and, during Joyce's time there, was a hotbed of Irish nationalism. Since his youth Joyce had been especially gifted with words and proficient with languages and liter-

Joyce, seen here around 1924 with a patch on his eye, began to experience serious trouble with his eyesight as early as 1915.

ature. When he was eighteen, he published a review of Ibsen's *When We Dead Awaken* in a prestigious London literary journal, the *Fortnightly Review.*

Ireland made stringent nationalistic demands on its writers during the decades preceding the 1916 Irish Rebellion. Every young Catholic Irishman was called on by the nationalists to do his utmost for the cause, and writers young and old were to turn their pens to the furtherance of their country's independence from the English. Joyce felt that his first duty was to his own freedom to create permanent literature and refused to participate in writing nationalistic propaganda for his country. His obligation as the eldest son—and the one with a university degree—to help the family in its poverty also weighed heavily on him. However, duty was not enough to keep him from going to Paris, where he had planned to study medicine but instead spent his time reading in the Sorbonne library.

The martello tower where Joyce spent six days in 1904. One of a chain of fortification towers built south of Dublin between 1809 and 1814, it forms the setting for the opening scene of *Ulysses.* The tower is now Ireland's Joyce Museum.

The Emerging Writer. Upon graduation in December 1902, Joyce left Dublin, having obtained some promises from W. B. Yeats and others to do some reviewing. He wrote some book reviews for the *Daily Express,* a Dublin newspaper, during this period in Paris, but he was never far from poverty and constantly wrote to family and friends in search of loans. He returned to Dublin in 1903, when his mother was dying, and by 1904 began a series of writing projects. They included a novel about a young artist not unlike himself, *Stephen Hero,* which later became *A Portrait of the Artist as a Young Man,* a collection of poems he called *Chamber Music,* and a series of short stories that would eventually be part of *Dubliners.* The first of the *Dubliners* stories, "The Sisters," was published in *The Irish Homestead* on August 13, followed by "Eveline" on September 10 and "After

the Race" on December 12. During this period he spent six days living with a medical student, Oliver St. John Gogarty, in a martello tower at Sandy Cove, south of Dublin. The tower was a fortification built to ward off invasions by the French but, as the site of the opening of Joyce's *Ulysses,* eventually became one of the major tourist attractions in Ireland.

Marriage and Family Struggles. On June 16, 1904, Joyce went out on his first date with Nora Barnacle, the woman who would emigrate with him from Ireland, live with him for the rest of his life, bear his two children, and finally legally marry him 26 years later in London. The June 16 date meant enough to Joyce that he immortalized it as the date his most respected novel, *Ulysses,* takes place. It is now celebrated all over the literate world as Bloomsday, after the name of its protagonist, Leopold Bloom.

Joyce was already fluent in French and Italian, and when he and Nora arrived in

Joyce (left) with his contemporaries, from left to right, American poet and critic Ezra Pound, English writer and editor Ford Madox Ford, and esquire John Quinn in Pound's studio in Paris in 1924. Pound, an enthusiastic entrepreneur of modern art, was instrumental in making sure Joyce's work found its way into the major literary circles of the day.

Zurich, he had expected to take a teaching job in the Berlitz school there. The position failed to materialize, but the Berlitz staff found him a position in Pola, Italy, where he learned German. After his expulsion, along with all other foreigners, from Pola, he went on to another Berlitz school and private language tutoring in Trieste. Except for a six-month hiatus in Rome, where Joyce took a job in a bank, Trieste remained his home for a decade. Joyce's son, Giorgio, was born on July 27, 1905, the same year Stanislaus, his brother, came to live with the family. By early the next year Joyce had begun a protracted struggle to have the short story collection, *Dubliners,* published. It eventually came out in 1915.

The Joyces' second child, Lucia Anna, was born July 26, 1907. As Joyce's heavy drinking became an increasing problem, Stanislaus did his best to help support the family, and Joyce's sisters Eileen and Eva both came from Dublin to help. Joyce's one commercial venture, the Volta Cinema, Dublin's first movie house, opened on December 20, 1909, and closed within a few months, while Joyce continued work on *Portrait of the Artist.*

In 1913 Yeats sent Ezra Pound a copy of "I hear an army charging upon the land," the concluding poem of *Chamber Music,* and Pound published it in his anthology *Des Imagistes.* When Joyce mailed Pound sections of *Portrait* and *Dubliners,* Pound arranged to have them published in *The Egoist,* through which Joyce gained entry into the leading literary circles of European modernism and acquired a generous benefactor in Harriet Shaw Weaver and another lifelong supporter in Sylvia Beach, the owner of Shakespeare and Company, a bookstore that was the center of avant-garde literature in Paris.

HIGHLIGHTS IN JOYCE'S LIFE

1882   James Augustine Aloysius Joyce is born on February 2 in Rathgar, Dublin, Ireland.

1888   Attends Clongowes Wood School.

1893   Enters Belvedere College.

1898   Enters the Royal University, Dublin.

1902   Graduates from the university; leaves for Paris.

1903   Returns to Dublin to be with his dying mother.

1904   Has first date with Nora Barnacle in June; they leave for Europe in September.

1905   Son, Giorgio, is born.

1907   Daughter, Lucia Anna, is born.

1909   Joyce starts Volta Cinema theater.

1914   Complete text of *Dubliners* is published.

1916   Complete text of *A Portrait of the Artist as a Young Man* is published.

1922   Complete text of *Ulysses* is published.

1931   Joyce legally marries Nora Barnacle.

1939   Complete text of *Finnegans Wake* is published.

1941   Joyce dies on January 13 and is buried in Zurich.

The Joyce family moved to Zurich in 1915, when World War I made Trieste uncomfortable for British subjects and Stanislaus was interned. By the time Joyce arrived in Zurich, he had already started writing *Ulysses*. Ezra Pound serially published completed chapters from 1918 to 1920 in *The Little Review*, and five more sections appeared in *The Egoist* in 1919.

The Joyces began receiving money from a number of public and private sources, and Joyce was finally able to give up teaching in 1920 and move to the scene of intellectual impetus, Paris. There, in 1922, after the first full edition of *Ulysses* was published by Shakespeare and Company, Joyce was surrounded by admirers, including many of the most prominent people in modern literature and the arts. Joyce's intemperance, however, coupled with poor eating habits, decaying teeth, and lifelong problems with his eyes, had left him with a number of serious impediments to his health. In addition, his daughter's mental instability was the source of considerable anxiety. Despite all of these tribulations, he began his longest, most daring, and critically controversial book, entitled only "work in progress" until it was published seventeen years later in its entirety in 1939 as *Finnegans Wake*.

World War II and the invasion of Paris caused the Joyces to flee Paris for unoccupied Vichy, and after nearly a year they finally gained readmission to neutral Switzerland and Zurich, where Joyce died of a perforated duodenal ulcer on January 13, 1941.

The Writer's Work

James Joyce's literary production consisted of miscellaneous poems, essays, and reviews, a largely unsuccessful play, *Exiles,* some fragments published posthumously, and his four major works. *Dubliners* is a collection of short stories, *A Portrait of the Artist as a Young Man* is a novel of youthful learning and initiation, and *Ulysses* deals principally with a protagonist approaching middle age. The fourth major work, *Finnegans Wake,* defies categorization. Its protagonist is HCE or, as he is dubbed in one incarnation, Here Comes Everybody, and its characters are both ancient and modern, young and old, all the people "down through Christian minstrelsy" largely interchangeable with a host of historical and modern popular culture figures.

Joyce Chooses His Audience. Joyce's motives for writing the kinds of work he did were as complex as the work he produced. Coming of age in Ireland, he felt his choices to

Joyce standing in the doorway with his publisher, Sylvia Beach, who owned and ran the famed Paris bookstore Shakespeare & Company, which became a popular gathering spot and haven for the *lost generation,* a term used to describe foreigners, mostly Americans, writing and living in Europe. Beach published Joyce's *Ulysses* when no English publisher would dare. The controversy surrounding this decision is richly reflected in the posters above and beyond Joyce (left) as he meets with Beach, his loyal and ardent lifelong supporter.

be either to write nationalistic propaganda to glorify the cause or to expose Ireland's weaknesses and the pettiness of its citizenry with very realistic accounts of the terms on which they existed and thus catch the conscience of his race. In an era of radical nationalism, Joyce had a love-hate relationship with his country. He could either knuckle under and enjoy the approbation of his countrymen or tell the truth as he saw it and gain their enmity and censure. He chose the latter course. It seemed clear to him that he would never be allowed to write the way he wanted to if he stayed in Ireland, and yet he was convinced that he had the makings of a great writer. So, like the Irish patriots whose convictions made them exiles from British-dominated Ireland, Joyce decided to live his life out in exile in Europe. He needed to live in a place that provided access to a more sophisticated international audience and admission to the intellectual and creative elite that was attempting to redefine history in modern terms.

Nevertheless, Joyce never lost touch with the country that had shaped his ideas and background. Ireland, particularly Dublin, is the subject matter and locale of all his fiction, and he wanted accuracy in everything he wrote. He would write to friends and relatives in Dublin for information about the physical settings in his books; for example, to find out how high the front railing was above the basement level at a certain address. He worked with a street map of Dublin, a copy of the June 16, 1904, *Irish Times,* and a book called *Thom's Directory,* which listed the names and addresses of all Dublin's citizens and businesses in order to maintain perfect accuracy in his works. When his characters bore the names of real people, printers sometimes refused to publish his works simply for fear of suits and reprisals.

The Complexity in Joyce's Work. This realism was framed within his encyclopedic knowledge of classical mythology, philosophy, ecclesiastical history and doctrine, literary history, popular culture, and music from street ballads and music hall songs to Wagnerian opera. Joyce's reading was both enormous and various. His Jesuit education acquainted him with classical, biblical, and ecclesiastical literature and the Latin needed to read it, and he haunted the public reading room of Dublin's National Library until he switched to the library in Paris. As might be expected, Joyce's works are replete with literary allusions, especially when he depicts the mind of his own surrogate character, Stephen Dedalus. When Joyce moves from Stephen to other characters with different reading habits, they provide allusions to a variety of other topics, including science, popular events, and sports, many related to Irish history, both contemporary and ancient. All such references are buried in the text of his books, and since most allusions are not readily apparent, except perhaps to someone who lived in turn-of-the-century Dublin, it took critics and scholars decades of research to produce volumes of explications of Joyce's allusions so that readers could better understand the complexity of meaning in even the simplest of his works. His *Dubliners* stories seemed for years to be fairly dull, matter-of-fact depictions of the lives of various people who lived in the city. They contained little in the way of plot and seemed more like snapshots of existence there. However, when scholars looked more closely at the repetitions and interweavings of scenes and motifs and began to gloss what most Irish Catholics knew almost by instinct about such institutions as the confessional, the mass, and Irish politics, the stories took on new and deeper meaning.

Experimentation and Innovation. Joyce's unique complexity gave birth to an army of Joyce scholars, now known as the "Joyce industry," who have sifted through his works for hidden clues, broadened the perception of his genius for all readers, and ultimately gained Joyce the international reputation for which he strove. In 2002 there were more publications on Joyce than any other single author in the English language except Shakespeare. Readers

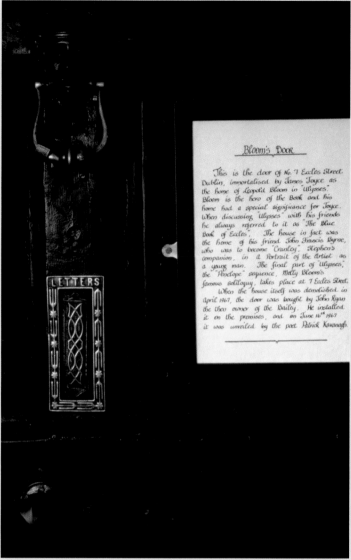

Bloom's Door

This is the door of No. 7 Eccles Street, Dublin, immortalised by James Joyce as the home of Leopold Bloom in 'Ulysses'. Bloom is the hero of the book and his home had a special significance for Joyce. When discussing 'Ulysses' with his friends he always referred to it as 'The Blue Book of Eccles'. The house in fact was the home of his friend John Francis Byrne, who was to become 'Cranley', Stephen's companion, in 'A Portrait of the Artist as a young man'. The final part of 'Ulysses', the 'Penelope' sequence, Molly Bloom's famous soliloquy, takes place at 7 Eccles Street.

When the house itself was demolished in April 1967, the door was bought by John Ryan the then owner of the Bailey. He installed it on the premises, and on June 16th 1967 it was unveiled by the poet Patrick Kavanagh.

Although Joyce lived outside Ireland for most of his life, his hometown of Dublin figures prominently in all his fiction. Fixated on crafting accurate descriptions of Dublin, Joyce often referred to sources other than his memory to ensure the authenticity of his details. Dubliners, too, are fixated on their native son. Tributes and references to Joyce can be seen all throughout Dublin. This statue of the Irish writer (above left) stands on the corner of O'Connell Street and Earl Street North in Dublin, while a framed document on the door of No. 7 Eccles Street (above) recounts the history of the famous address, which was immortalized as the home of Leopold Bloom in Joyce's *Ulysses.* These two gentlemen (left) celebrate "Bloomsday," June 16, by tracing the route of the fictional Leopold Bloom through the streets of Dublin in 2001, almost eighty years after the publication of the novel that brought Bloom to life.

often have to put a lot more effort into understanding his work, but those willing to do so reap far greater rewards for their efforts.

That said, Joyce's two earlier books connect with most readers on a personal level without benefit of professional explication. His experimentation with narrative was less dramatic in them, even though the way in which his fiction was narrated did contain the modernist innovation of having the language of the narration mimic the mind-set of the character under discussion. Thus, in describing the action of a character, Joyce often uses the sort of terminology the character himself would use, not only creating a description of the action but subtly influencing the reader's interpretation of both the character and what he or she believes. Often these passages produce a comic effect.

While there is plenty of humor in *Dubliners,* what use of comedy there is in his autobiographical novel, *A Portrait of the Artist as a Young Man,* is muted, the product of a serious young writer's way of looking at things. As he progressed through midlife (his own and his protagonist's), Joyce's tone and temper took a decidedly comic turn. *Ulysses* begins with an essentially comic character, Buck Mulligan, bantering with the serious Stephen Dedalus/Joyce and hilariously mocking Stephen for his earlier humorless devotion to his self-proclaimed vocation as high priest of art. Nine episodes (chapters) later, Stephen admits in the library scene that he no longer believes his own ingenious arguments, and Joyce begins to turn the book increasingly toward comic exaggeration, style mimicry, and incongruous ideas, as *Ulysses* evolves into one of the great comic novels in literary history.

Joyce's last book, *Finnegans Wake,* is a novel that draws its name from an Irish American comic song about a hod carrier who dies in a fall from a ladder and comes back to life at his own wake when some whiskey is accidentally poured on his mouth. Joyce's story of fall and resurrection is comic throughout. Nearly every word is in a sense resurrected, composed of multiple meanings and similar-sounding words derived from scores of foreign languages, names, and quotations. The book, when read aloud, adds yet another dimension of comic ambiguity by orally combining words, familiar quotations, and song lyrics with each other to form puns. Some consider the importance of *Finnegans Wake* to derive from the very idea that it is one enormously long joke. Even if it were, Joyce spent seventeen years of intensive labor (both his and a score of editorial assistants') writing it.

The jury is still out on the worth of the novel, but it provides for many who attempt to read it a lasting sense of delight. To read even a single page is a broadening, enriching, and liberating experience.

BIBLIOGRAPHY

Attridge, Derek. *The Cambridge Companion to James Joyce.* Cambridge, UK: Cambridge University Press, 1990.

Begnal, Michael H., ed. *Joyce and the City: The Significance of Space.* Syracuse, NY: Syracuse University Press, 2002

Beja, Morris, and David Norris, eds. *Joyce in the Hibernian Metropolis: Essays.* Columbus, OH: Ohio State University Press, 1996.

Bowen, Zack, and James F. Carens, eds. *A Companion to Joyce Studies.* Westport, CT: Greenwood Press, 1984.

Ellmann, Richard. *James Joyce.* New York: Oxford University Press, 1982.

Fargnoli, A. Nicholas, and Michael Patrick Gillespie. *James Joyce A to Z: The Essential Reference to the Life and Work.* New York: Oxford University Press, 1995.

Hayman, David. *Ulysses: The Mechanics of Meaning.* Englewood Cliffs, NJ: Prentice-Hall, 1970.

Joyce, Stanislaus. *My Brother's Keeper: James Joyce's Early Years.* New York: Viking, 1958.

Kenner, Hugh. *Dublin's Joyce.* London: Chatto and Windus, 1956.

Magill, Frank N., ed. *Magill's Survey of World Literature.* Tarrytown, NY: Marshall Cavendish, 1993.

Morse, J. Mitchell. *The Sympathetic Alien: James Joyce and Catholicism.* New York: New York University Press, 1959.

Rice, Thomas Jackson. *James Joyce: A Guide to Research.* New York: Garland, 1982.

Tindall, William York. *A Reader's Guide to James Joyce.* New York: Octagon Books, 1959.

Poetry and Exiles

Two publications of James Joyce that are comparatively unfamiliar to readers other than Joyce specialists are his suite of 36 poems, *Chamber Music,* and his play, *Exiles.* Joyce's real genius was for writing fiction, and his poetry and drama did little to enhance his stature as one of the century's greatest writers. Nevertheless, these works do reveal something about the ways his creative mind worked and much about what directions he would eventually take in his writing.

Poetry. In all, Joyce published 782 lines in 52 poems, including two suites, or collections, *Chamber Music* (1907) and *Pomes Penyeach* (1927). The better-known *Chamber Music* appeared in a sequence that was arranged by Joyce's brother Stanislaus to tell a sort of story. According to William York Tindall, who edited the 1951 version for Columbia University Press,

> The thirty-six poems tell a story of young love and failure. At the beginning the lover is alone. He meets a girl and their life, after suitable fooling, is almost successful. Then a rival intrudes. The hero's devotion gives way to irony and, at last, despair. Alone again at the end, the lover goes off to exile (*Chamber Music,* p. 41).

The poems resemble Elizabethan love lyrics. They are so musical that Joyce even wrote actual music for several to be sung, and most if not all have since been set to melodies by at least 142 various composers, some with Joyce's active collaboration and encouragement. The second source from which Joyce drew inspiration is the biblical Song of Solomon. Both subject matter and allusion in the poetry confirm that the suite was the product of a young but precocious poet expressing his first love and jealousy in terms of classic verse and the biblical allusions that were a part of his extensive religious education. The poetry is a lot closer to Joyce's own thinking than the heavily satiric and ironic distance he keeps in his prose.

Joyce saw rivals everywhere. Despite his feigned self-assurance and confidence, he was often wary of those who would either seek to bring him to heel or to win the affections of his lover/wife. Part of his egomaniacal identification with martyred sainthood was the ever-present danger of betrayal. The name of his autobiographical surrogate, Stephen Dedalus, is a combination of the first Christian martyr and the fabulous inventor Daedalus, who fashioned a set of wax wings to escape the island of Crete. Someone who thinks of himself in terms of a saint, a creative genius, and a martyr must be ever wary of rivals and betrayers, and Joyce was most vulnerable to betrayal on the sexual level; a jealous person might steal his lover away at any time. This predisposition, along with his

This depiction of Joyce by an unknown artist offers the viewer a rare and intimate look at Joyce's left side, the side of his face rarely seen in public photographs. The one-dimensional portrait personifies the confidence and self-assurance for which Joyce is so well known without providing so much as a hint of any vulnerable aspect of his personality.

lover/wife's physical attractions, made sexual betrayal and paranoia a real possibility. When Joyce was on a visit back to Ireland, he heard from a lying confidant that Joyce's then common-law wife had had an affair with a friend of Joyce, and Joyce reacted with near hysteria. It took some time before the lie was exposed and things came back to normal, but the threat of infidelity continued to affect Joyce, and it became a major ingredient in *Ulysses*.

Exiles. From its early thematic development in the poetry through its increasingly comic presence in Joyce's last two novels, the threat of inconstancy appears in Joyce's work, but never is it so close to what Joyce supposed as a reality than it is in his only play, *Exiles*. Joyce's protagonist, Richard Rowan, is a writer who returns with his wife and son to Ireland after years in Italy. His rival is a longtime friend, Robert Hand, a successful Dublin literary figure who has become infatuated with Richard's wife, Bertha. Richard arranges a clandestine meeting between his rival and his wife in order to test his wife's fidelity and his own endurance and reactions. Richard's professed motives for putting himself and his wife through the mental agony of the assignation are complex and both masochistic and sadistic. The issue of whether carnal infidelity actually occurs is never resolved, despite scene after scene of confessions by one character to another regarding their feelings and what actually happened. In the end the audience is left, as are the characters, with doubt about what happened and what to make of it.

It seems fairly clear that Joyce was working through his own marital problems and doubts with his play and that he was not able to retain enough distance between his fictional characters and his own situation, as he had been able to do in *Portrait of the Artist* and *Ulysses*. This supposition is born out by a set of notes he appended to the printed version of *Exiles*, notes that relate to the play but are as much a reflection of his own state of mind as of those of the characters in the play.

There are many complexities in the play that have not been recounted in this brief skeletal synopsis. Joyce, in writing *Exiles*, was heavily influenced by his early passion for Ibsen, whose cause he had championed against popular opposition from both priests and students at his university in Dublin. Although he was imitating the sort of realistic drama found in Ibsen's *When We Dead Awaken*, Joyce so infused *Exiles* with his own problems that he may have lost his objectivity and his detachment from the action.

Exiles, although never a complete artistic failure, was hardly high drama, and the audiences that were drawn to it simply because Joyce wrote it never fully appreciated the long conversations and self-analyses by the characters. The play seemed destined for relative obscurity until Harold Pinter's production of it in London in the 1970s played to enthusiastic audiences. As a consequence of this production, *Exiles* was recognized by some to be a far better drama than anyone had ever given it credit for being. Bernard Benstock writes that the Pinter version was set as a period piece "in an almost exaggerated Edwardian atmosphere . . . [a]ll the lines were read with precise politeness . . . and no suggestion of Joycean irony was permitted in the interpretation" (*A Companion to Joyce Studies*, pp. 361–362).

Pinter's version caused Joyce scholars to reevaluate Joyce's only play; the jury is still out, however. The question is whether Joyce really intended his work to be interpreted the way Pinter handled it or whether Joyce would have been more satisfied with the earlier productions over which he had some influence. At the heart of the dilemma is the difference between the arts of music and drama on the one hand and the art of writing fiction on the other. Nothing stands between the reader and the printed page in fiction, and the reader interprets the work for him- or herself. Music and drama require intermediaries—with music, instrumentalists, conductors, and vocalists, and with drama, actors, directors, and technical people. All interpret what the writer said and how it is to be retold or replayed or sung. Thus, the final receptors, members of the audience,

Charles Hunt's nineteenth-century painting *The Two Suitors* unveils the demoralizing and sinking discovery that one must contend with another for a beloved's affections and illustrates one of Joyce's greatest fears, the fear of losing his beloved to another. Joyce claimed that his attractive wife, Nora, a chambermaid from Galway who lacked his education and background, made him a man.

must base their own interpretations of a given work on individual performances by the intermediaries. Coming to grips directly with Joyce's fiction by reading it is not the same as seeing all of the nuances of a novel crammed into a 90-minute-long dramatic interpretation. Even Shakespeare's plays are different on the printed page from what they are on stage or in film. While Pinter may be responsible for a laudable interpretation of Joyce's work, if the work itself does not meet the same standards that apply to the rest of the Joyce canon, one might be justified in being disappointed at Joyce's attempt at dramatic writing.

SOURCES FOR FURTHER STUDY

Benstock, Bernard. "*Exiles*, Ibsen and the Play's Function in the Joyce Canon." *Forum* 11 (1970): 42–52.

Bowen, Zack. "*Exiles*: The Confessional Mode." *James Joyce Quarterly* 29 (Spring 1992): 581–586.

Kenner, Hugh. "Joyce's *Exiles*." *Hudson Review* 5 (1952): 389–403.

Reader's Guide to Major Works

DUBLINERS

Genre: Short stories
Published: London, 1914
Time period: 1890s–1903
Setting: Dublin, Ireland

Themes and Issues. Joyce set out to depict, as realistically as possible, the everyday lives of a variety of average Dublin citizens, using actual city settings and intermixing real people with fictional creations to create a montage of sometimes grim, sometimes funny struggles against poverty, frustration, religion, politics, alcoholism, and parental abuse.

Publication Problems. Joyce's references to real people and events and his unsparing descriptions of the Catholic Church and the political institutions of his day led one publisher after another to reject the book. One accepted and then canceled publication even after Joyce had agreed to change some of the language in order to pacify indignant printers. In all it took nine years of negotiations before Grant Richards, the publisher who had first agreed to publish the volume and then refused, reconsidered and finally published *Dubliners.*

Plots, Structure, and Design. The collection includes 15 stories, the first 11 arranged in chronological order according to the relative ages of their protagonists. Then there are three more representing the chief influences on Dublin life—politics, the arts,

and the Church—and a longer concluding story that touches on the themes developed in the earlier stories. This last story, "The Dead," is the most widely read and most likely to be accessible to first-time Joyce readers.

The first three stories, "The Sisters," "An Encounter," and "Araby," are the only ones told in the first person, all three by their young protagonists. The unnamed boys are progressively older, as their attitudes indicate. "The Sisters"

A child's admiration for his refined uncle in Domenico Ghirlandaio's fifteenth-century painting *Vecchio col nipotino (Old Man with Nephew)* echoes the adoration and respect Ireland's Catholic youth were taught to have for the clergy. In his short story "Sisters," the opening story in his 1914 collection of short stories, *Dubliners,* Joyce challenges a young boy, and the reader, to consider the possibility that flaws may exist in the Catholic Church.

deals with a boy's relation to the Church in the guise of the old priest who is his tutor. "An Encounter" is about a boy's relationship to the secular world of his companions and a "queer old josser" who bears some vague similarity to the priest in the first story. The final story in this initial group, "Araby," concerns a boy's crush on a girl he sees as an inspirational figure, his romantic trip to a fair to bring her back a gift, and his disillusionment when the romantic quest turns sour.

The second group, "Eveline," "After the Race," "Two Gallants," and "The Boarding House," deals with various young but as yet unmarried people. The last of these is about a young clerk who is seduced by the daughter of a boardinghouse matron and, is about to be forced by her calculating mother and a righteous priest into a shotgun marriage as reparation. "A Little Cloud" tells the story of a young would-be poet stuck as a clerk behind a desk, scorned by his wife, and besieged by a bawling child. "Counterparts" picks up another version of married life with yet another clerk, whose manhood is so threatened he has turned to drink and to beating his own pleading son.

The next two stories deal with single middle-aged people. "Clay" is the touching story of a simple but romantic spinster's Halloween visit to the family of a man whom she had once cared for in his childhood, and "A Painful Case" details the plight of an opinionated bachelor who had missed his chance of companionship with a married woman whose death may have been ultimately caused by his rejection of her.

The "public" stories in *Dubliners* begin with "Ivy Day in the Committee Room." In this tale the political hacks who work for a candidate they know is no good piously lament the loss of integrity in Irish politics, even though they themselves have helped to bring it about. "A Mother" is about the political promotion of a piano accompanist by her stage mother. In midconcert the mother balks at having her daughter continue the second half because the pianist's remuneration has come up short. "Grace" relates the tale of a group of drinkers who attempt to spiritually rehabilitate one of their own by taking him to a religious retreat to hear a platitudinous sermon.

The last story, "The Dead," concerns the disillusionment of an egotistical writer, not unlike Joyce himself, who has remained in Ireland instead of migrating. He discovers after a party that his wife has had a love relationship with a young man willing to die for her. Seeing the story of the young lovers as a contrast with his own self-centered relations with his wife and his country, the writer turns it into a beautiful national narrative of sacrifice.

Connections, Allusions, Metaphors, and Narrative Technique. Like Joyce's novels, the short stories have little in the way of a plot. Each is about a character locked into an individual set of circumstances from which there is apparently little opportunity to escape. Nevertheless, there is a point to representing a particular segment of life in each story. That point may or may not be recognized by the protagonist, or the protagonist may have a false recognition.

The idea of recognizing an underlying truth—that is, having an epiphany (a sudden revelation)—is, as a literary expression, one of the great contributions Joyce made to modern literature. In some of the stories, the characters never achieve an epiphany, while in others they come to a false revelation, leaving the reader to discover the meaning of the events independent of whatever conclusions the characters have made.

Joyce does not leave his readers completely in the dark. He plants clues in the story and allows readers to decide for themselves whether the clues affect the story's meaning. For instance, in the first story, "The Sisters," which concerns the relationship between a young boy and a retired priest, the old priest tries to teach the boy some of the more complicated Church doctrines. When the old man dies, the boy attends his wake. In the first paragraph of the story, three words occur to the boy, *paralysis, gnomon,* and *simony.* They appear to have no connection with any event in the text. The

SOME INSPIRATIONS BEHIND JOYCE'S WORK

When Joyce was a young man, Ibsen was his hero; he even studied Norwegian to read Ibsen in the original (Ibsen had a strong and not entirely salutary influence on Joyce's play, *Exiles*). The technique of stream of consciousness, so crucial to an understanding of *Ulysses* and *Finnegans Wake*, was first employed by the French novelist Édouard Dujardin (1861–1949) in his novel *Les Lauriers sont coupés* (The Laurels Are Cut Down, 1888); Joyce freely admitted to lifting the technique from Dujardin. Curiously, Dujardin's style was an attempt to re-create in prose the "endless melody" and interior monologues of his great hero, the German composer Richard Wagner (1813–1883). Joyce loved Wagner, too, and he was not immune from the great composer's influence.

The medieval philosophers Thomas Aquinas and Giordano Bruno also had much to do with the formation of Joyce's mind, but in many ways the most remarkable impact came from the Italian philosopher Giambattista Vico (1668–1744), whose cyclic theory of history not only impressed Joyce on its own account but also dovetailed neatly with Joyce's well-established predilections for recurrence and circularity. Lastly, the dream psychology of Sigmund Freud (1856–1939) had evident influence on all of Joyce's work—it, too, undoubtedly had strong temperamental appeal for Joyce. In a sense, all of these influences may be found on display on the very first page of *Finnegans Wake*; in the cases of Vico and Wagner, the references are direct and unmistakable, and they function not at all unlike a tip of the hat from one artist to others he admires.

priest, however, was a paralytic; simony, the buying and selling of ecclesiastical offices, was an illicit moneymaking practice common in but condemned by the medieval Church; and both terms may have been linked in the boy's mind with some sort of corruption connected with his teacher. The fact that Joyce mentions that the word *gnomon* (what remains of a parallelogram when a smaller parallelogram is removed from it) was taken from Euclidean geometry provides thereby the clue that only a shell remains when some part of the original religious meaning is taken away. At the wake one of the priest's sisters tells the story of how the priest's laughing in an empty confessional led to his forced retirement from the parish. It seems that the scene may be connected to the priest's relationship to the boy and that it might have involved the paralysis of the now hollow gnomon of Roman Catholicism and its corruption (simony). The reader can merely speculate on the meaning of the three words, either in the story or in *Dubliners* as a whole, but at least one of the three ideas suggested by the words can be applied in some way to every one of the stories as well as to the collection in its entirety.

The chronology described above is only one link connecting the stories. Allusions to ideas, situations, and events abound throughout the collection, but each recurrence is so buried in the events of the stories following that, like the above example from "The Sisters," it might easily be overlooked. The goal of Joyce scholarship is to uncover the deeper meanings throughout.

The last story, "The Dead," brings the whole collection full cycle, back to the first story, "The Sisters." Both stories are about sisters, and both deal with the relationship of the living Irish to the dead who preceded them, all now covered by the snow falling all over Ireland, "upon all the living and the dead." The last biblical-

Reflecting "The Dead," the last story in Joyce's *Dubliners,* the living and the dead converge amidst the same blanket of snow in Caspar David Friedrich's 1810 painting *Graveyard in Snow.* As in Joyce's "The Dead," neither the living nor the dead are sheltered from the white blanket and the thoughts of the living are never far from those who have gone before them.

sounding proclamation is delivered by Gabriel, a man named after an archangel, about his dead rival, Michael (also named after an archangel), who, Christlike, gave up his life for love of a woman that, in her husband's eyes, appears to be a symbol of Ireland. Whether she was or not, Joyce allows the reader to decide.

SOURCES FOR FURTHER STUDY

Beja, Morris, ed. *James Joyce: "Dubliners" and "A Portrait of the Artist as a Young Man": A Casebook.* London: Macmillan, 1973.

Gifford, Don, and Robert J. Seidman. *Joyce Annotated: Notes for "Dubliners" and "A Portrait of the Artist as a Young Man."* Berkeley: University of California Press, 1982.

Hart, Clive, ed. *James Joyce's "Dubliners": Critical Essays.* New York: Viking, 1969.

Torchiana, Donald T. *Backgrounds for Joyce's "Dubliners."* Boston: Allan & Unwin, 1986.

A PORTRAIT OF THE ARTIST AS A YOUNG MAN

> **Genre:** Novel
> **Subgenre:** Novel of initiation
> **Published:** New York, 1916
> **Time period:** Late nineteenth and early twentieth century
> **Setting:** Dublin, Ireland

Themes and Issues. *Portrait of the Artist* concerns the childhood and young manhood of a would-be writer whose history closely resembles Joyce's own. While the reader may be tempted to make a complete identification between Joyce and his protagonist, it must be realized that he took liberties with autobiographical facts when doing so suited his purpose. A long fragment of his first draft of the novel, published as *Stephen Hero* years after Joyce's death,

The resolute pose on a jagged landscape in Caspar David Friedrich's 1818 oil painting *The Wanderer above the Sea of Clouds* embodies the daring of Joyce's autobiographical protagonist as he bravely embraces his decision to embark on his future as an artist in Joyce's 1916 novel, *Portrait of the Artist as a Young Man.*

more closely presents Joyce's own experiences and thoughts than did the revised manuscript that became *Portrait*. Joyce's protagonist in *Portrait* emerges with ironic detachment.

All the scenes in the book are acted out in the presence of the protagonist, Stephen Dedalus. Often the reader is not told directly what Stephen makes of these events and is left to conjecture what they might mean to him. Again, what is unspoken is very important in shaping the mind of the young artist, but the reader has to supply the explanations of how Stephen is affected. Why and how the scenes described are important to the whole portrait of the budding artist is left largely for the reader to discern.

In the last chapter a couple of long monologues by Stephen set forth his aesthetic theories, his ideas about his role as a writer, and his potential contribution to the history of the Irish race. How and why he arrived at these positions the reader can reconstruct through an understanding of the events Stephen has experienced during the course of the novel and their psychological effect on Stephen's thinking. His eventual decision to leave Ireland in order to get on with his role as a writer is not announced until the last pages of the book. By that time the reader knows that Stephen has felt, since his days at Clongowes, that he is different from the other boys and that he identifies with such past heroes as Christ, Satan, and the martyred political leader Charles Stuart Parnell. He does not want to become a priest, although the vocation was offered to him at Belvedere, but in priestly fashion he would like to change the commonplaces of life into immortal poetry as the priest changes bread and wine into the body and blood of Christ. He will take his own life as his subject matter and, as priest-author, will turn it into eternal literature. So he becomes "a priest of eternal imagination" as both sacrificer and sacrificed, producing deathless art. His love for a young girl, who has for him become both a temptress and the inspiration of his art, is the subject of his poem about her temptation, the only artwork he produces during the course of the novel.

If all the constraining shackles imposed on him—to be manly, patriotic, religious, and a responsible provider for his family—are to be thrown off, Stephen, like his creator, Joyce, has no alternative but to leave Ireland to pursue his career. So, at the end, it is with both trepidation and bravado that he packs his clothes for the journey to Europe and his future.

SOURCES FOR FURTHER STUDY

Feshbach, Sidney. "A Slow and Dark Birth: A Study of the Organization of *A Portrait of the Artist as a Young Man.*" *James Joyce Quarterly* 4 (1967): 289–300.

Kershner, R. B., Jr., ed. *A Portrait of the Artist as a Young Man: The Complete, Authoritative Text with Biographical and Historical Contexts, Critical History, and Essays from Five Contemporary Critical Perspectives.* New York: Bedford Books/St. Martin's Press, 1993.

Scholes, Robert, and Richard Kain, eds. *The Workshop of Daedalus: James Joyce and the Raw Materials of "A Portrait of the Artist as a Young Man."* Evanston, IL: Northwestern University Press, 1965.

Schutte, William M. *Twentieth-Century Interpretations of "A Portrait of the Artist as a Young Man": A Collection of Critical Essays.* Englewood Cliffs, NJ: Prentice/Spectrum, 1968.

POETRY	PLAY	NOVELS
1907 Chamber Music	1918 Exiles	1916 A Portrait of the Artist as a Young Man
1927 Pomes Penyeach		1922 Ulysses
	SHORT FICTION	1939 Finnegans Wake
	1914 Dubliners	

ULYSSES

Genre: Novel
Subgenre: Chronicle of urban life
Published: Paris, 1922
Time period: June 16, 1904
Setting: Dublin, Ireland

Structure. *Ulysses* is divided into eighteen episodes, or chapters, each focused on specific locales of Dublin and progressing through one day, beginning in the morning and ending in the early hours of the next morning. The action follows the activities and thoughts of two characters: Stephen Dedalus, the protagonist of Joyce's earlier *Portrait,* and Leopold Bloom, a 38-year-old advertising salesman, who has a sensual wife, Molly, and a teenage daughter, Milly, now working in a photography shop in another town.

The major model for the action is Homer's travel epic, the *Odyssey,* in which perhaps the archetypal hero in Western literature,

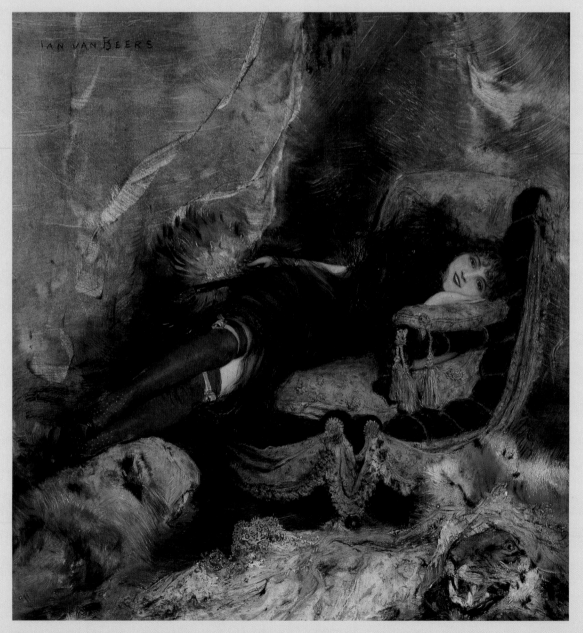

The flirtatious woman in Jan van Beers's oil painting *The Courtesan* represents the coquettishness of Molly, Leopold Bloom's unfaithful wife, in Joyce's 1922 novel, *Ulysses.* The betrayal of women in general is a significant theme in all of Joyce's major works.

Odysseus—renamed Ulysses by the Romans-travels around the known world in a 10-year epic journey following the Trojan War. His goal is to return home and regain sovereignty over his family and estates. Naming his chapters in his manuscript only, Joyce patterned them loosely after characters or episodes from the *Odyssey.* Joyce grafts the story of the heroic Ulysses onto Leopold Bloom, an ordinary, nondescript citizen, and by association transforms the activities of everyday Dublin life into a seriocomic representation of what heroism really means in a commonplace existence. Bloom's wife, Molly, far from being Odysseus's faithful wife, Penelope, engages in adultery during the day, and Bloom, knowing how she is spending her time that afternoon, does nothing to prevent it and may even vicariously enjoy the prospect. Stephen Dedalus becomes a surrogate for Odysseus's son, Telemachus, but rejects the offer to spend the night with the Blooms and perhaps replace their son, Rudy, who died as a young child.

At its end, *Ulysses,* unlike the *Odyssey,* holds no promise of any permanent solutions to the Blooms' problems. Nor are the Blooms represented as a couple who will live happily for the rest of their lives. However, there is in this homecoming story a sense of modern survival and a belief that, despite all its largely unrewarding reality, life can be funny and even contain moments of genuine heroism.

Ulysses/Bloom. Bloom is not particularly heroic, but neither is he pitiful. He is sustained by the simplest enjoyments—pleasant moments of elimination in the outhouse, eyeing a woman's ankles as she lifts her skirts—and he is comfortable with his tendencies toward masochism and fetishism. He is also moved by the plight of people less fortunate than he and has any number of social and economic schemes for the general good. Some are farfetched, but others make good practical sense. Like his would-be son, Stephen, Bloom even thinks he may someday write something himself but mostly for the money it might bring rather than out of any hope of a more-than-fleeting immortality.

Bloom is not a typical Irishman. He has a Jewish father, a Christian mother, and a Roman Catholic wife. As a Jewish-Irish citizen that does not drink heavily, he takes a lot of abuse and never completely fits into the company of his hard-drinking, anti-Semitic contemporaries. He reads a lot on various scientific and social topics and tries to fit into a lower-class male social company that is far less tolerant of his semilearned philosophical observations than concerned about whether he buys the next round of drinks. He is also kind and humane and on occasion stands up for what he believes.

Publication Problems. In this novel Joyce opened modern literature to subjects, espe-

A newly discovered manuscript, seen above, of the "Circe" chapter, the chapter in which Bloom and Stephen Dedalus meet in *Ulysses,* sold at Christie's auction house in New York on December 14, 2000, for $1,546,000, the highest price ever paid for a James Joyce manuscript. The new owner is the National Library of Ireland.

cially sex and elimination, that many thought were so scandalous that they should never be printed, and once again Joyce's work ran up against censorship—by publishers, printers, prosecutors, and leagues for the suppression of various vices. Publication in Paris was one thing, but even after the book's phenomenal success on the Continent, it took 12 more years and one of the most famous censorship battles in history before Random House was finally able to publish it in 1934 in the United States. It was still banned in Ireland until the last quarter of the twentieth century.

Innovations in Language and Style. The first 10 of the 18 episodes in *Ulysses* are written in what the critic Michael Groden described as the "initial style," using combinations of words as single words, for example, "graveclothes" and "threadbare cuffedge." More dramatically, Joyce varies the narrative voice between a third-person narrator and the direct stream of conscious thought of one of the characters, usually Stephen or Bloom. Thus, the reader has both an outside, objective point of view and an internal, subjective one. The initial difficulty is often to separate what the author is trying to say about something from what the character is thinking about it. Joyce does not indicate with any of the usual signifiers, such as quotation marks, who is saying what, and the result is an effect that blends reality with perception—which, after all, is how people understand things anyway. The technique was not entirely original with Joyce, but he took it further than anyone else had at the time and developed a unique sense of reality in his prose.

Other narrative innovations become more blatant as the episodes progress. They begin in earnest with the musical devices Joyce inserts in his "Sirens" episode. The chapter opens with a verbal overture consisting of snippets of sentences and songs taken from the episode as a whole. Each chapter from "Sirens" on has a unique form of narration. For example, "Oxen of the Sun," parodies literary prose styles from Anglo-Saxon to contemporary dialects. As the writing grows more daring in its parodies, it also gets funnier. What began as a mildly humorous, realistic novel progresses into a rollicking comedy, although one that never completely loses its serious intent.

SOURCES FOR FURTHER STUDY

Bowen, Zack. *"Ulysses" as a Comic Novel.* Syracuse, NY: Syracuse University Press, 1989.

Gifford, Don, and Robert J. Seidman. *"Ulysses" Annotated.* Berkeley: University of California Press, 1988.

Lawrence, Karen. *The Odyssey of Style in "Ulysses."* Princeton, NJ: Princeton University Press, 1981.

McCarthy, Patrick A. *"Ulysses": Portals of Discovery.* Boston: Twayne, 1990.

Tucker, Lindsey. *Stephen and Bloom at Life's Feast: Alimentary Symbolism and the Creative Process in James Joyce's "Ulysses."* Columbus: Ohio State University Press, 1984.

FINNEGANS WAKE

Genre: Epic novel
Subgenre: Encyclopedic comedy
Published: New York, 1939

The Title. By the time *Finnegans Wake* was finally published in its entirety under its present name, bits and pieces had already appeared in print under various section titles. Seventeen years in the making, it had already attracted a large audience of Joyce followers, many of whom were to be disappointed because they could not understand much of anything in the long, complicated book. It appears to be written in words that sound like English but have traces of dozens of foreign words that form unique combinations.

The combination of words extends to a multiplicity of characters and events centered around the mythic character of Finn MacCool, the giant ur-Irishman whose bed was Dublin. His feet were at one end of the bay, and his head lay across the bay at Howth. He is identified with Tim Finnegan, the hero of the ballad "Finnegan's Wake." Tim dies but is resurrected, as Joyce resurrects the legend of Finn MacCool. However, the title of the book tells the reader a lot more. First, it hints that the book is, in

The play of shadow in the background and fresh paint in the foreground seems to imply the passage of time and, with that, a history of funerals in Harry Epworth Allen's twentieth-century painting *Funeral in Connaught*. With the same all-encompassing style, Joyce, too, excludes no one and speaks to everyone in his 1939 epic novel Finnegans Wake.

brief, about all of everything: life is composed of an endless series of repetitions. When he is resurrected, Finn will be Finn again. (Of course, "Finn again" is a homonym of "Finnegan.")

In the title there is no apostrophe in the word *Finnegans,* so it is not merely one Finnegan but all Finnegans who awaken or whose deaths are celebrated with an Irish wake, resurrection, or both. Also, the term *wake* can be either a noun, as when one attends a wake, or it can be a verb, part of a command to all Finnegans to wake up. These puns in the title suggest what Joyce has in mind for all the rest of the words in a book where nearly every word or phrase has multiple meanings.

Names. The name of the protagonist is Humphrey Chimpden Earwicker, or Here Comes Everybody, or anyone else whose name begins with the letters *H, C,* and *E.* He is married to an equally ubiquitous wife. *ALP* stands for Anna Livia Plurabell, in one incarnation the river Liffy, who/which runs through Dublin. She is called the Bringer of Plurabilities, that is, multiple meanings and identifications. The couple has two sons, Shem and Shaun, who are perennial rivals, and a daughter, Issy, both a reincarnation and a rival of her mother. The fluidity of the characters and their many transmutations resemble those of a dream, although whose dream it is or how many dreamers there are is still a matter of debate among *Wake* scholars.

Joyce said that it had taken him seventeen years to write *Finnegans Wake* and that there was no reason why scholars should not spend their lives reading it. There are so many characters in the book that Aldeline Glasheen has published three book-length censuses of *Wake* in an attempt to identify them all, along with her famous essay, "Who's Who When Everybody Is Somebody Else." One category of allusions that make up the *Wake* is the more than 2,000 references to the titles and lyrics of songs, and Joyce scholars are certain to unearth more over time. Scores of books pretend to have discovered the key to the *Wake*, and each year more theories and explications appear.

Approaches. Most Joyce critics agree that *Finnegans Wake* has to be read aloud to be fully appreciated and that above all it is a long, complicated, and exceptionally funny game. It often presents echoes or approximations rather than snapshots of specifics and should be read for its verbal virtuosity and pure enjoyment value rather than for any profundity hidden in the text. There have been many attempts by other writers, artists, and musicians to replicate Joyce's impressionistic style in *Finnegans Wake* and still more to explain what it is about, but the *Wake* remains probably the strangest book of the century and certainly the most problematic.

SOURCES FOR FURTHER STUDY

Begnal, Michael H., and Fritz Senn, eds, *A Conceptual Guide to "Finnegans Wake."* University Park: Pennsylvania University Press, 1974.

Benstock, Bernard. *Joyce-Again's Wake: An Analysis of "Finnegans Wake."* Seattle: University of Washington Press, 1965.

Bishop, John. *Joyce's Book of the Dark: "Finnegans Wake."* Madison: University of Wisconsin Press, 1986.

Campbell, Joseph, and Henry Morton Robinson. *A Skeleton Key to "Finnegans Wake."* New York: Viking, 1966.

McHugh, Roland. *Annotations to "Finnegans Wake."* Baltimore: Johns Hopkins Unversity Press, 1991.

Tindall, William York. *A Reader's Guide to "Finnegans Wake."* New York: Farrar, Straus & Giroux, 1969.

Resources

Major collections of Joyce's manuscripts and letters in the United States are at the State University of New York at Buffalo, the University of Texas at Austin, Cornell University, Yale University, Southern Illinois University at Carbondale, and the Rosenbach Museum in Philadelphia. The largest depository of Joyce material in Ireland is at the National Library in Dublin.

International James Joyce Foundation. This foundation, housed at Ohio State University, maintains a Web site that cross-lists other Joyce Web sites with chat rooms on specific Joyce works and national and international activities (http://www.cohums.ohio-state.edu/english/organizations/ijjf/).

Publications. The principle Joyce serial publications in the United States are *The James Joyce Quarterly*, published at the University of Tulsa; *The James Joyce Literary Supplement*, published at the University of Miami; and *The James Joyce Annual*, published by the University of Texas at Austin.

ZACK BOWEN

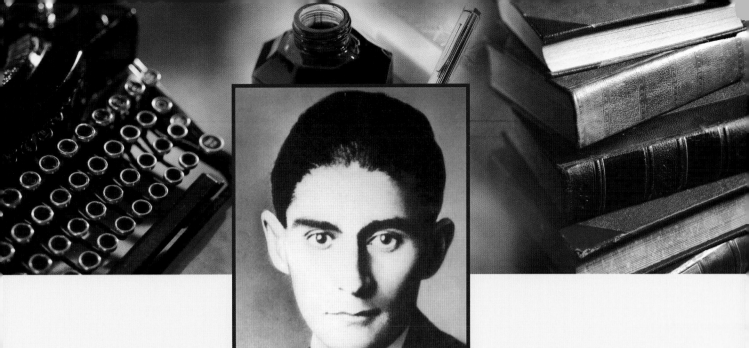

Franz Kafka

BORN: July 3, 1883, Prague, Czechoslovakia
DIED: June 3, 1924, Kierling, near Vienna, Austria
IDENTIFICATION: Early-twentieth-century German-Jewish writer whose enigmatic stories and novels transformed modern literature.

SIGNIFICANCE: Franz Kafka could never have imagined the enormous impact that his writing would have on the generations of readers and writers that followed him. At his death only a fraction of his writing had been published, and he was unknown outside a small circle of friends and literary enthusiasts. Twice before his death, he asked his closest friend, the novelist Max Brod, to destroy all remaining manuscripts, including three unfinished novels, his diaries and letters, and scores of short stories and sketches. But for the disobedience of Brod, who chose to publish and promote them, the world would never have discovered the rich complexity of Kafka's imagination. Thanks to his unequaled ability to dramatize the anxieties and ambiguities of modern life, his writing has come to epitomize the modern era in Western literature.

The Writer's Life

Franz Kafka was born on July 3, 1883, in a small house on the old town square near the edge of the Jewish ghetto in the Austro-Hungarian city of Prague (now the capital of the Czech Republic). Though of Jewish descent, his parents, Hermann and Julie (née Löwy) Kafka, maintained only a perfunctory relationship to their religion, and Franz was raised in language and culture as a German. Named after Emperor Franz Josef, Kafka had three sisters, Gabriele (Ellie), Valerie (Valli), and Ottilie (Ottla), and two brothers who died in infancy.

Childhood. Kafka spent much of his early childhood alone or in the care of nurses. He was four when his first brother, Georg, died from measles in 1887. Heinrich, born that same year, died in 1888 of otitis. Of his early years Kafka wrote to Felice Bauer in 1912: "Thus for a very long time I was all alone, forever battling nurses, aging nannies, snarling cooks, morose governesses, because my parents spent all their time in the shop." Kafka's perception of his childhood, recorded in greater depth in "Brief an den Vater" ("Letter to His Father"), conveys an early sense of oppression and isolation. The most significant aspect of Kafka's early childhood was his complicated and painful relationship with his father.

The Father. Hermann Kafka, the son of a butcher, rose from extreme poverty to establish a successful dry goods store in Prague. He was a domineering and practical man before whose physical and emotional strength Kafka cowered, in his life as well as his writing. In "Letter to His Father," Kafka describes an early childhood memory that left a deep and lasting psychological impression. In response to Kafka's repeated cries for a glass of water one evening, his father fetched him from his bed and locked him outside on a balcony. "Even years afterward," he wrote, "I suffered from the tormenting fancy that the huge man, my father, the ultimate authority, would come almost for no reason at all and take me out of bed

The young Kafka is seen here in an undated photograph with his right hand resting on the head of a dog. Kafka, a timid and obedient student, did well in school and was liked and respected by his teachers.

Kafka's parents, Hermann and Julie, are seen here in an undated photograph. Kafka considered his father an awesome, admirable, and repulsive tyrant and felt that he identified more with his maternal ancestors, although he was not particularly close to his mother either. In spite of his strained relationship with his parents, he lived with them most of his adult life.

in the night and carry me out onto the *pavlatche* [balcony]." Kafka's letter, written at the age of 36, describes the extraordinary impact that his father had on his emotional and psychological development. There is no evidence that Kafka's father ever read it.

Education. At the age of six, Kafka enrolled in the Deutsche Knabenschule, a German elementary school for boys. His father hoped that a German education would put him in a better position to secure respectable employment, as German was the official language of business and politics at the time. Kafka later attended the state-run Altstädter Gymnasium, a highly competitive secondary school, before enrolling at the German Karl-Ferdinand University in 1901. He spent two weeks studying chemistry and briefly considered a degree in German studies before settling on law.

Early Writings. Kafka began writing at an early age, though virtually nothing remains of this work. In a letter to Oskar Pollack, a classmate at the gymnasium to whom he sent several stories and sketches, Kafka describes his early writing as "high-flown stuff" and himself as "mad about grand phrases." Even as an adolescent, he wrote and staged plays for his parents on their birthdays, enlisting his three sisters as actors. Only one early story, "A View from a Window," escaped destruction.

The Prague Circle. During his high school and university years, Kafka became acquainted with several classmates who played important roles in his intellectual development. This group included Hugo Bergmann, Ewald Pribram, and Oskar Pollack, with whom Kafka developed a close attachment. At the German university, Kafka attended the German

HIGHLIGHTS IN KAFKA'S LIFE

1883 Franz Kafka is born July 3 in Prague.

1889–1893 Attends German primary school for boys.

1893–1901 Attends Altstädter Gymnasium.

1896 Celebrates his bar mitzvah on June 13.

1902 Meets Max Brod.

1906 Receives doctorate in jurisprudence from the German Karl-Ferdinand University in Prague.

1907–1908 Is employed by the Assicurazioni Generali, an Italian insurance company.

1908 Begins work at the Workers' Accident Insurance Institute.

1909 Publishes two dialogues from "Description of a Struggle" in the literary magazine *Hyperion;* publishes "The Aeroplanes of Brescia" in the Prague newspaper *Bohemia.*

1910 Publishes short sketches in *Bohemia* that will appear later in *Meditations.*

1911 Vacations in Switzerland, Italy, and Paris; meets small Yiddish theatrical troupe in Prague.

1912 Meets Felice Bauer; begins his novel *Amerika;* writes "The Judgment."

1913 Publishes *Meditation,* a small volume of sketches; "The Judgment" appears in Max Brod's literary annual, *Arkadia;* Kafka publishes "The Stoker," the first chapter of *Amerika;* writes "The Metamorphosis."

1914 Announces official engagement to Felice Bauer; begins writing *The Trial;* writes "In the Penal Colony."

1915 Publishes "The Metamorphosis"; wins the Fontane Prize for "The Stoker"; moves into his own rented room.

1917 Is diagnosed with tuberculosis; makes final break with Felice Bauer; publishes "A Report to an Academy" in *Der Jude.*

1918 Writes "The Great Wall of China."

1919 Meets Julie Wohryzek; publishes *A Country Doctor,* a collection of short stories; writes "Letter to His Father"; begins correspondence with Milena Jesenká-Polak.

1920 Publishes "In the Penal Colony"; visits a sanatorium in Meran, Austria; meets Milena in Vienna.

1921 Visits a sanatorium in the Tatra Mountains; meets Robert Klopstock.

1922 Begins work on *The Castle;* retires from the insurance company in June; publishes "A Hunger Artist" in *Die Neue Rundschau.*

1923 Writes "Investigations of a Dog," "The Burrow," and "Josephine the Singer"; meets Dora Diamant and moves to Berlin; is bedridden in December with fever.

1924 Stays at the Sanatorium Wiener Wald; tuberculosis spreads to his larynx; in May Kafka enters Hoffmann Sanatorium in Kierling near Vienna; dies on June 3 and is buried in the Jewish cemetery in Prague on June 11.

Student's Reading and Discussion Hall, where he met Max Brod, who would become his lifelong friend and literary executor. An informal literary circle was formed, which included the novelists Felix Weltsch and Franz Werfel and the dramatist Oskar Baum. The group, the Prague Circle, met regularly to discuss literature and philosophy. They attended readings, frequented cafés and bars, and gathered to read from their own writings. In contrast to his later fastidious isolation, Kafka enjoyed a healthy and socially active university life.

Prague. In a letter to Oskar Pollak in 1902, the 19-year-old Kafka described his native city this way: "Prague does not let go. Neither of us. This little mother has claws." Kafka lived most of his life in Prague in his parents' home, and his relationship to the city was enigmatic. He walked frequently through its streets, used it as a background for some of his writing, and always desired to escape its stifling closeness. In a diary entry from 1914, he writes, "To get out of Prague. Against the most severe human injury that has ever befallen me, to act with the strongest antidote at my command."

The Advocate. Kafka received his law degree on June 18, 1906, and was obligated to practice law for one year as a prerequisite for employment in civil service. Though he had no real passion for the law, he viewed it as a practical though uncomfortable choice of professions. The law allowed him the widest latitude in selecting a future career that would facilitate his desire to write.

Hermann Kafka's dry goods store in the 1930s. The second *n* in *Hermann* is missing on the door. Both of Kafka's parents spent a lot of time at the shop, and neither understood why their son felt the need to document his inner world through writing.

Civil Service. In 1908 Kafka took a position with the Assicurazioni Generali, an Italian insurance company in Prague. The strain of a long work day, often lasting twelve hours, left him little time to write, and after two months he began looking for another job. Through the influence of a former classmate's father, he obtained a position at the Arbeiter-Unfall-Versicherungsanstalt, the Workers Accident Insurance Institute, where he would remain a respected and proficient employee for the next 14 years. He worked from 8:00 in the morning to 2:30 in the afternoon, a schedule that left his evenings free for writing.

Kafka posing with his first fiancée, Felice Bauer. Their first engagement was broken in July 1914, when Kafka realized that he could not be both a writer and a husband to Bauer. They became officially engaged for the second time in July 1917, but the engagement was broken again by December of that year. Kafka stated that his diagnosis with tuberculosis was the reason.

The Frustrated Writer. Kafka published his first writing, a small piece taken from an early story, "Description of a Struggle," in 1908 in the literary magazine *Hyperion*. Two more sections of the story appeared in *Hyperion* in 1909. Despite this modest but respectable success, Kafka discovered numerous obstacles to his writing. His work at the insurance institute was a constant distraction, as was his family, with whom he still lived. In 1911 Kafka agreed to work temporarily in the afternoons at his cousin's asbestos factory. This work left him exhausted and unable to write in the evenings.

Felice Bauer. Kafka met Felice Bauer on August 13, 1912, at the home of his friend Max Brod and began a passionate correspondence with her that would last until 1917. With the exception of occasional personal visits, Kafka's love affair with Felice was a literary one. He wrote hundreds of letters in which he pleaded for her love, analyzed the nature of his writing, and ultimately argued his own unfitness for marriage. The two were engaged twice, but Kafka could never bring himself to marry. Felice, like most of the women who Kafka loved, was sacrificed for the sake of his writing, a pursuit that he could never reconcile with married life.

A Breakthrough. On September 22, 1912, Kafka spent the night writing at his desk. By the morning he had completed "The Judgment," a short story about a young man's confrontation with and ultimate defeat by his father. In a diary entry dated September 23, 1912, Kafka wrote, "Only in this way can writing be done, only with such coherence, with such a flinging open of body and soul." The experience invigorated him. In 1913 he published *Meditation*, a collection of short stories and sketches, and he was awarded the Fontane Prize in 1915 for "The Stoker," the opening chapter of his novel *Amerika*. Having found his stride as a writer, he quickly completed many of his most accomplished works of fiction, including "The Metamorphosis" (1913), "In the Penal Colony" (1914), "The Great Wall of China" (1917), and portions of two novels, *The Trial* and *Amerika*.

Judaism. In 1912, after many years of ambivalence, Kafka began to demonstrate an interest in his Jewish heritage. His diary records his avid reading of several books on Jewish history and Jewish-German literature. A small Yiddish theatrical troupe visited Prague during 1911 and 1912, and Kafka attended many of its performances. He wrote letters of introduction for the troupe and appealed to Zionist organizations to sponsor performances and readings. He also organized a solo reading at the Jewish town hall in Prague for his friend the chief actor in the troupe, Yitzak Levi, for whom Kafka delivered an introductory lecture. Though Kafka's relationship to Judaism remained primarily an intellectual and emotional one to the end of his life, he made considerable progress in his study of Hebrew and even considered moving to Palestine on several occasions.

Tuberculosis. Kafka suffered for much of his life from nightmares, migraines, insomnia, and indigestion. Numerous diary entries reveal an almost obsessive concern for his health, which he always felt was failing. To combat this fear, he maintained a strict vegetarian diet and often spent his vacations in various natural health sanatoriums. In 1917 he suffered a hemorrhage in his lungs and was diagnosed with tuberculosis. From that time forward, though he often experienced periods of relative ease, his health began to decline.

The Final Years. Battling chronic fatigue and rapidly deteriorating health, Kafka struggled to keep writing. He finished several short stories, including those collected in *A Hunger Artist*, and became engaged briefly to Julie Wohryzek, a dressmaker from Prague. In 1919 he began a correspondence with Milena Jesenká-Polak, who eventually translated his works into Czech. The two fell in love and met on a few occasions in Vienna, but Milena was unwilling to

A manuscript page from Kafka's much acclaimed 1915 short story, "The Metamorphosis."

leave her husband. Tuberculosis forced Kafka to retire from the insurance institute in 1922. That same year, during a trip to Silesia in northern Bohemia, Kafka began work on *The Castle*.

While recuperating at a resort on the Baltic Sea in 1923, Kafka met Dora Diamant, the daughter of a rabbi. He moved to Berlin to live with her, and they made preliminary plans to live in Palestine. He studied Hebrew and continued to write despite his deteriorating condition. By December 1923, he was bedridden with fever, and in March 1924, he returned to Prague, where he discovered that tuberculosis had spread to his larynx. He received medical treatment in the Sanatorium Wiener Wald and finally in a sanatorium in Kierling, near Vienna, where Dora and Robert Klopstock, a young medical student he had met in 1921, nursed him. On June 3, 1924, a month shy of his forty-first birthday, Franz Kafka died.

The Writer's Work

In a letter to Felice Bauer in 1913, Franz Kafka described the nature of his work as a writer. "My whole being is directed toward literature; I have followed this direction unswervingly . . . and the moment I abandon it I cease to live." He called this type of being *Schriftstellersein,* or "being as a writer," and his attempt to live in or through his writing was an effort to achieve a level of truthfulness, an authentic existence that he could accomplish in no other way. In his writing, Kafka strove, as he states in his diary, to "raise the world into the pure, the true, the unchangeable." That most of his works are incomplete testifies to the difficulty of the task that Kafka set before himself. The paradox of the one who seeks what cannot be attained—or in Kafka's case, the one who writes what cannot be contained in language—informed most of Kafka's texts.

Issues in Kafka's Fiction.

Characters in Kafka's fiction exist in an almost perpetual state of bewilderment as a result of their confrontation with people, institutions, or parts of themselves that defy their understanding. Guilt, fear, and alienation from oneself and others also play critical roles in the motivations of Kafka's characters. In a letter to Milena Jesenká-Polak, Kafka described his own inner fear as "perhaps the best part" of him, and added, "This fear is after all not my private fear—it is simply that too, and terribly so—but it is as much the fear of all faith since the beginning of time." At stake for Kafka as a writer and for his characters as literary extensions of himself is the pursuit of an irreducible meaning and a certainty that what one seeks actually exists and can be attained.

People in Kafka's Fiction.

Many of Kafka's characters, such as Josef K. in *The Trial* and the surveyor K. in *The Castle,* are thinly disguised portraits of himself. He also created numerous animal characters to embody the alienation and despair that marked his private life. In "A Report to an Academy," an ape explains to a group of scientists how he came to mimic the behavior of human beings. The burrow in the story of the same name finds his ideal home underground, though threatening and unknown creatures surround him. Perhaps the best-

Max Brod, Kafka's longtime friend and fellow writer, was instructed by Kafka to continue the work that Dora Diamont, Kafka's companion for the last year of his life, had begun—burning his manuscripts. Brod, ignoring Kafka's wishes, instead published all of Kafka's remaining works, diaries, and letters after his death.

known character in Kafka's fiction is Gregor Samsa, the traveling salesman who wakes up to discover that he has become a giant insect.

Kafka's Literary Legacy. In the years following Franz Kafka's death, Max Brod persisted in his effort to publish and keep in print all of Kafka's works, which were at various times banned in Germany and Czechoslovakia. Following their translation into English, his books created a stir in post–World War II America, and his reputation as a unique and prophetic writer gained international momentum. Authors as varied as Gabriel García Márquez and Albert Camus acknowledged their debt to Kafka. The novelist and literary critic Vladimir Nabokov hailed him as "the greatest German writer of our time," and he has been almost universally acclaimed as the leading force behind the modernist movement in literature and as a kind of spokesman for humanity in the twentieth century.

In "Hope and the Absurd in the Work of Franz Kafka," collected in *The Myth of Sisyphus*, Albert Camus wrote: "The whole art of Kafka consists in forcing the reader to reread." Whether or not this is the whole of Kafka's art is disputable. What is beyond dispute is the enormous influence he has had on generations of readers, authors, and critics, who have discovered in the intense isolation and inner conflict of his characters a reflection of their own experience.

FILMS BASED ON KAFKA'S WRITING

1963 *The Trial*

1968 *The Castle*

1970 *The Penal Colony*

1976 *The Metamorphosis*

1984 *Amerika (released in the United States as* Class Relations, *1984)*

1987 *The Metamorphosis (TV, United Kingdom)*

1993 *The Trial*

BIBLIOGRAPHY

Alter, Robert. *Necessary Angels: Tradition and Modernity in Kafka, Benjamin, and Sholem.* Cambridge, MA: Harvard University Press, 1991.

Beck, Evelyn Torton. *Kafka and the Yiddish Theater.* Madison: University of Wisconsin Press, 1971.

Brod, Max. *Franz Kafka: A Biography.* New York: Schocken, 1947.

Citati, Pietro. *Kafka.* New York: Knopf, 1990.

Deleuze, Gilles, and Felix Guattari. *Toward a Minor Literature.* Vol. 30, *Theory and History of Literature.* Minneapolis: University of Minnesota Press, 1986.

Flores, Angel, and Homer Swander, eds. *Franz Kafka Today.* Madison: University of Wisconsin Press, 1958.

Greenberg, Martin. *The Terror of Art: Kafka and Modern Literature.* London: André Deutsch, 1971.

Karl, Frederick. *Franz Kafka: Representative Man.* Boston: Ticknor and Fields, 1991.

Pawel, Ernst. *The Nightmare of Reason: A Life of Franz Kafka.* New York: Farrar, Straus and Giroux, 1984.

Politzer, Heinz. *Franz Kafka: Parable and Paradox.* Ithaca, NY: Cornell University Press, 1966.

Robert, Marthe. *As Lonely As Franz Kafka.* New York: Harcourt Brace Jovanovich, 1982.

Rolleston, James, ed. *A Companion to the Works of Franz Kafka.* New York: Camden House, 2002.

Humor in Franz Kafka's Short Fiction

Max Brod, Kafka's first biographer and intimate friend, drew early attention to an overlooked element in Kafka's fiction. "Even the most gruesome episodes in Kafka's writing," Brod wrote in his biography, "stand in a curious twilight of humor, an investigator's interest and tender irony." Brod further claimed that those who knew Kafka only through his writing could not appreciate the marked difference between his personal demeanor among friends and acquaintances and his brooding literary self as depicted in his writing. "There was no end to our joking and laughing—he liked a good, hearty laugh, and knew how to make his friends laugh, too." Something of this playfulness among friends exists in his writing as well, though the "hearty laugh" is replaced by humor of an entirely different sort. Kafka's humor resembles the laughter of the Odradek in "The Cares of a Family Man," a laughter that "has no lungs behind it" and sounds like "the rustling of fallen leaves."

Kafkaesque. Kafka's ability to depict the world in unusual and terrifying ways has insinuated itself into the English language as the adjective Kafkaesque. "The world becomes Kafkaesque," writes Frederick Karl in *Franz Kafka: Representative Man,* "when it relocates the individual in areas he or she could not have preconceived; when it redefines the terms of existence in unforeseen modes." Such existential upheavals, as Gregor Samsa's transformation into an insect in "The Metamorphosis," provided Kafka with an opportunity to explore their comic, as well as tragic, implications. Gregor's behavior following his transformation becomes increasingly grotesque, even comical. He hides under the sofa. When excited, he scurries in all directions, across the floor, the walls, and the ceiling. In the final section of the story, he becomes entranced by the music of Grete's violin. Gregor betrays a lingering humanity that makes his actions as an insect incongruous, comical, and in the end, tragic.

Animal Stories. Several of Kafka's short stories feature animal protagonists, a device that allows Kafka to relocate familiar themes in unfamiliar and humorous contexts. In "Josephine the Singer," a mouse meditates on the art of the singer Josephine, whose vanity ultimately sets her at odds with her people. An ape describes his ascent to manhood following his capture by hunters in "A Report to an Academy." The ape, called Red Peter because of a scar on his cheek, tells the academy that his adoption of human speech and mannerisms provided a way of escaping his captivity. He tells how he went on to achieve fame for his accomplishments as a variety show performer, though he was often criticized for dropping his trousers for private visitors to exhibit the gunshot wounds that he received when he was captured.

The easy smile on Kafka's face in this photogragh, taken around 1920, seems to suggest that he did indeed have a sense of humor and helps support the theory that he purposely tempered even the gloomiest of his stories with an ethereal and absurd wit that reflects the ridiculousness in human nature. It has been said that Kafka and his listeners often burst out laughing during his readings.

Melodrama. A grim tale of a father's condemnation of his son, "The Judgment" also exhibits elements of melodrama and farce. The father, initially perceived to be a peaceful and soft-spoken invalid, transforms himself suddenly from a frail and neglected old man wearing soiled undergarments into a thundering giant who jumps on his bed and shakes his dressing gown in mockery of Georg Bendemann's fiancée. In the face of his father's attack, Georg can think of nothing but the fact that his father has pockets even on his bedclothes. The exaggerated gestures of the father, as he prances on his bed and calls his son a comedian, contrast sharply with his previous submissiveness. Like Gregor Samsa in "The Metamorphosis," Georg cannot initially comprehend his changed position with regard to his father, and he suffers a tragic death.

Parables and Myths. Many of Kafka's shorter works are written as parables, wherein he exploits the limitations of human knowledge. "Before the Law," which was written as a part of his novel *The Trial,* was published separately dur-

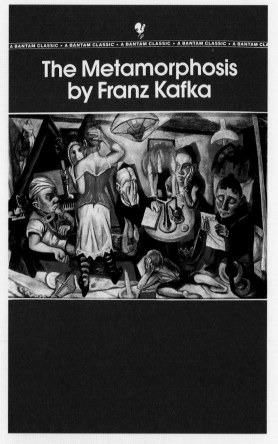

This cover adorned the Bantam's 1986 edition of "The Metamorphosis", Kafka's classic tale of alienation and despair.

ing his lifetime and depicts a man's frustrated attempt to gain access to the law. "An Imperial Message," originally part of the story "The Great Wall of China," describes a messenger's hopeless attempt to deliver a message from a dying emperor. Kafka also reinvents mythological and historical characters. In "Poseidon," the sea god becomes an encumbered administrator whose clerical work keeps him from enjoying his watery domain. In "The New Advocate," Kafka envisions Alexander the Great's noble horse, Bucephalus, as an advocate in the law courts.

In his story "On Parables," Kafka describes the nature of parables as an attempt to express what is essentially inexpressible. The liberties he takes in refashioning myths and historical figures is, on a certain level, an act of subversion by which he illustrates the insufficiency of these methods for transmitting truth. The images he conjures are often humorous, for example, a horse entering a court building or Poseidon complaining about his job. The images can also be troubling, as is the image of the half kitten, half lamb in the story "A Crossbreed," whose divided nature makes it long for death.

Kafka's home at 22 Golden Lane in Prague. Kafka found it hard to break away from his hometown of Prague, although he claimed he wanted to. He once wrote of it, "This little mother has claws."

Conclusions. In *Kafka's Narrators,* Roy Pascal describes Kafka's humor as ambiguous in effect, "so that we are not certain whether there is true humour present and whether what has the appearance of humour does not simply intensify the horror." Kafka's dark visions of human alienation, of fragmented identities, and of the impenetrable mystery that seems to engulf reality may seem antithetical to any comic interpretation. Kafka punctuates his stories, however, with a playfulness derived from unusual narrative contexts and the folly of human behavior that seems inappropriate and inexplicable in the given situation. Behind these devices stands the author, whose nervous laughter, hollow and ominous like that of the Odradek, is necessary to preserve some sense of power over the despair that informed so much of his life and work.

SOURCES FOR FURTHER STUDY

Kafka, Franz. *The Complete Stories.* Edited by Nahum Glazer. New York: Schocken Books, 1971.

Karl, Frederick. *Franz Kafka: Representative Man.* New York: Ticknor and Fields, 1991.

Pascal, Roy. *Kafka's Narrators: A Study of His Stories and Sketches.* New York: Cambridge University Press, 1982.

Reader's Guide to Major Works

THE TRIAL

> **Genre:** Novel
> **Subgenre:** Allegory
> **Published:** 1925 (in English, 1937)
> **Time period:** Early twentieth century
> **Setting:** Unspecified urban setting

Themes and Issues. The world that Kafka conjures in *The Trial* is one of few rational explanations and one where a feeling of claustrophobia adds to the mounting terror of a criminal process that lacks any semblance of justice. The few physical manifestations of the court appear in overheated attics where the air is virtually unbreathable. Josef K.'s pursuit of the meaning of his trial, which takes him beyond the normal channels of human, judicial, and even divine assistance, compels the reader to experience his fractured sense of reality as he experienced it. In the end, the reader, like the executioners, acts as a witness to the spectacle of the shame that Josef K. fears will outlive him.

The Plot. Josef K., a respected bank employee with a promising future, wakes on the morning of his thirtieth birthday and discovers that he has been arrested. He is given no explanation of the charge against him. When he tries to confront the mysterious court by which he has been accused, an inexplicable community of shadowy judges and court clerks who operate in the dusty attics of labyrinthine apartment buildings, he gets no closer to understanding the nature of his trial.

His initial skepticism regarding the proceedings against him soon gives way to self-doubt as

This 1888 lithograph by Tom Merry captures a distracted, yet somehow authoritative-looking, group that is seemingly waiting for something to happen but not really caring about what it is. The group embodies the nonsensical and unjust system that determines Josef K.'s fate in Kafka's 1926 novel, *The Trial*.

he attempts to prepare a defense against an unknown charge. He enlists the help of a lawyer, whose descriptions of the court's operations increases his despair over his case. Believing that he can best represent himself, he dismisses the lawyer and works feverishly to prepare a petition that will convince the court of his innocence.

In a cathedral, where he has come to give a tour for a visiting bank client, Josef K. meets a priest who belongs to the court. The priest, a prison chaplain, informs him that his trial is going badly. He relates a paradoxical story of a man who tries to gain admittance to the law. After hearing the story, Josef K. begins to see the futility of his efforts to defend himself

against what he perceives as a deceitful and corrupt court. In the end, two court officials come to his room to deliver his sentence. They escort him to a quarry outside of town, place him on a stone block, and plunge a butcher's knife into his heart, bending over him as he dies to witness the verdict.

Analysis. A theatrical quality surrounds much of the action in *The Trial*, as though Josef K.'s life had suddenly become the subject of a farcical drama. When his executioners arrive in the final chapter, he is prepared for them. He wears black and pulls on his gloves "with the look of someone expecting guests." He calls

SOME INSPIRATIONS BEHIND KAFKA'S WORK

Kafka's greatest works of fiction dramatize a sense of alienation that exists at the very core of his characters' being, a perpetual state of otherness that cannot be overcome and that produces an infinite and unappeasable sense of guilt. The pattern for this fragmented consciousness can be found in Kafka's own experience as the son of an authoritarian and manipulative father and in his ambiguous cultural identity as a German-speaking Jew in the increasingly hostile Czech nationalist environment of Prague. Like Gregor Samsa in "The Metamorphosis" and Karl Rossmann in *Amerika,* Kafka was adrift in a family and a society that offered no real place for him, no sense of belonging.

Kafka also drew inspiration from the many books of fiction, poetry, biography, and travel and the diaries and letters that were his constant companions from an early age. In a letter to Felice Bauer in 1913, Kafka listed the Austrian poet and dramatist Franz Grillparzer and the novelists Fyodor Dostoyevsky, Heinrich von Kleist, and Gustave Flaubert as "four men I consider to be my true blood relations." He also read works by Czech authors, including Bozena Nemcová's *Babièa (The Grandmother),* published in 1855. In his biography of Kafka, Max Brod cited Kafka's lifelong love of the book and suggested that it was a possible inspiration for some of the events in Kafka's *The Castle.*

In 1911 a small Yiddish theatrical group visited Prague and performed a series of plays at the Café Savoy. Kafka attended these performances regularly and developed close relationships with the actors in the troupe. Numerous scholars have identified strong dramatic elements in Kafka's writing and suggest that his experience with the theatrical group inspired a new approach to his writing. He indeed demonstrated a new confidence, beginning in 1912 with the completion of "The Judgment." He also began to explore his Jewish heritage, an interest that gave him a link to a long tradition of storytellers and provided a rich source of inspiration.

them "old supporting actors" and asks, "Which theater are you playing at?" The terrifying subject of this drama is Josef K., whose very existence stands under judgment. Because he cannot understand this crucial point, his attempts to defend himself simply reinforce his guilt. This guilt, an inherent quality in Josef K. that has no perceivable source and no limit, is always present. Everyone he meets appears to be connected with the court and therefore with his guilt. As he lays under the executioners' knife, even death cannot release him from the shame of his sentence.

SOURCES FOR FURTHER STUDY

Citati, Pietro. *Kafka.* New York: Knopf, 1990.

Greenberg, Martin. *The Terror of Art: Kafka and Modern Literature.* London: André Deutsch, 1971.

Politzer, Heinz. *Franz Kafka: Parable and Paradox.* Ithaca, NY: Cornell University Press, 1966.

THE CASTLE

   Genre: Novel
   Subgenre: Allegory
   Published: 1926 (in English, 1930)
   Time period: Early twentieth century
   Setting: Unspecified rural village in northern Bohemia

Themes and Issues. Kafka employs the familiar theme of rootlessness in *The Castle,* though with an important difference that distinguishes the novel from his other writings. The surveyor K. is not compelled to penetrate the mystery of the castle. Unlike Karl Rossmann in *Amerika,* he is not banished from home and family. He chooses his fate, in the face of enormous obstacles, and pursues the castle with a dogged but clumsy determination. The German title of the novel, *Das Schloss,* carries a double meaning: *Schloss* means both "castle" and "lock." What K. seeks is precisely what is not open to him. Yet he persists in attempting to gain admittance where he is not welcome or invited.

The Plot. In the middle of an evening snowstorm, the narrator of the story, K., arrives in a small rural village. He is a surveyor by trade and hopes to find work at Lord Westwest's castle. The villagers are concerned about the surprise arrival of a stranger, and when K. falls asleep before the fire at the Bridge Inn, the innkeeper wakes him and insists that he leave. A phone call to the castle first refutes and then supports K.'s claim that his arrival was expected. Though still suspicious of him, the innkeeper provides K. with a room.

The following morning K. discovers that he cannot reach the castle from the main road. He decides to find someone in the village who might assist him in reaching the castle. His repeated attempts to find a guide who will lead him to his goal end in failure. The two assistants who arrive from the castle are incompetent and oppressive. The villagers as a whole cannot advise him on matters relating to the castle. The barmaid Frieda, whom K. eventually falls in love and lives with, first in the inn and later in the schoolhouse, leaves him. He is never able to contrive a meeting with Klamm, the castle official in charge of land surveying.

Having exhausted most of his resources, K. receives a message from Erlanger, one of Klamm's secretaries, instructing K. to meet him at the Herrenhoff Inn near the castle. However, K. is delayed by a chance meeting with another secretary, Bürgel, whom he discovers in one of the inn's rooms. Bürgel talks to him through the night and suggests that his assistance could help K. achieve his goal. Overcome by fatigue, K. falls asleep at the moment when he is on the verge of success. When he wakes, Bürgel dismisses him, and K. meets Erlanger in an adjoining room. Erlanger informs him that Frieda's return to the bar, which she had abandoned to be with him, would help his cause, but Frieda has already left him to resume her employment at the bar. The innkeeper finds K. in the corridor and leads him to the taproom, where K. finally succumbs to sleep.

Kafka never completed the final chapter of the novel, which reveals K.'s growing exhaustion from his pursuit of information about the castle and its officers. Max Brod claimed that Kafka intended to end the novel with K.'s

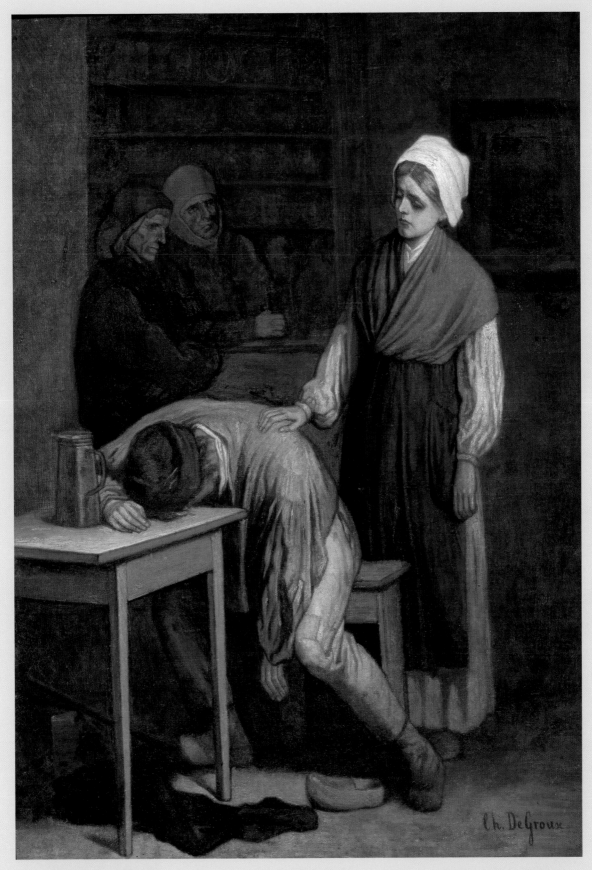

The exhaustion and disillusionment of the male figure in Charles de Groux's painting *The Drunkard* mimics Kafka's character K., his alter ego, in Kafka's final and unfinished novel, *The Castle*. K., hopelessly entangled in a web of bureaucratic inefficiency, misses every opportunity for any real progress.

death, after which his entrance to the castle would finally be granted.

Analysis. *The Castle* is widely considered to be Kafka's most mature and complex work of fiction, with numerous symbolic layers that have inspired a daunting body of critical literature. It is also his most autobiographical work. He began the narrative as a first-person account but later revised it. The central image of the castle as the ultimate source of a higher order of meaning has led many interpreters to cast K.'s pursuit of it as a religious quest. The castle also invites comparisons to the truth that Kafka tried to achieve in his writing. What seems evident is that K.'s quest, and ultimately Kafka's, is an existential one, the achievement of a foundation that legitimizes one's being and that provides, like the work of a surveyor, an accurate measure of reality.

SOURCES FOR FURTHER STUDY

Citati, Pietro. *Kafka.* New York: Knopf, 1990.

Greenberg, Martin. *The Terror of Art: Franz Kafka and Modern Literature.* London: André Deutsch, 1971.

Politzer, Heinz. *Franz Kafka: Parable and Paradox.* Ithaca, NY: Cornell University Press, 1966.

THE METAMORPHOSIS

Genre: Short story
Subgenre: Allegory
Published: 1915 (in English, 1936)
Time period: Early twentieth century
Setting: Unspecified urban setting

Themes and Issues. One of Kafka's best-known stories, "The Metamorphosis" combines elements of fantasy, tragicomedy, and an unsettling realism in its depiction of Gregor Samsa's alienation from his family and, ultimately, from himself. Though Kafka is always

LONG FICTION

1925   Der Prozess (The Trial, 1937)
1926   Das Schloss (The Castle, 1930)
1927   Amerika (America, 1938; Amerika, 1946)

SHORT FICTION

1913   Der Heizer: Ein Fragment (The Stoker: A Fragment, 1985)
1913   Betrachtung (Meditation, 1948)
1915   Die Verwandlung (The Metamorphosis, 1936)
1919   Ein Landarzt: Kleine Erzählungen (A Country Doctor: A Collection of Fourteen Short Stories, 1945)
1924   Ein Hungerkünstler: Vier Geschichten (A Hunger Artist, 1948)

1931   Beim Bau der Chinesischen Mauer: Ungedruckte Erzählungen und Prosa aus dem Nachlass (The Great Wall of China and Other Pieces, 1933)
1946   Erzählungen (The Complete Stories, 1971)
1948   The Penal Colony: Stories and Short Pieces
1952   Selected Short Stories

NONFICTION

1948–1949 The Diaries of Franz Kafka
1951   Tagebücher, 1910–1923 (Diaries)
1952   Briefe an Milena (Letters to Milena, 1953)
1953   Hochzeitsvorbereitungen auf dem Lande und andere Prosa aus dem Nachlass (Dearest

Father: Stories and Other Writings, 1954; also known as Wedding Preparations in the Country, and Other Posthumous Prose Writings
1958   Briefe, 1902–1924 (Letters)
1967   Briefe an Felice (Letters to Felice, 1974)
1974   Briefe an Ottla und die Familie (Letters to Ottla and the Family, 1982)

mindful of the power of symbols, he avoids abstraction by presenting Gregor's transformed self in vivid detail, as an accomplished fact, in the opening sentence of the story. In doing so, the effect of his metamorphosis precedes the cause, and the reader's understanding of the source of his altered state runs parallel to Gregor's own understanding.

The Plot. After an uneasy night's sleep, Gregor Samsa, a commercial traveler, wakes to discover that he has been transformed into an insect. He is initially troubled by the transformation, though he soon turns his thoughts to more practical matters. A look at the clock reminds him that he has overslept and must hurry if he is to catch his train. When a clerk from his office arrives to inquire about his absence, Gregor hurls himself out of bed and opens his bedroom door. His appearance horrifies the clerk, who tries to flee. Thinking that he must explain that his predicament is only temporary, Gregor chases after him, only to be driven back into his bedroom by his father.

Following this first banishment from the family room, Gregor keeps to his own bedroom. His sister Grete, though terrified of him,

brings him food each day and straightens the room. When he begins to crawl on the walls and ceiling, Grete clears away the furniture to give him more room to move. In time Gregor ventures out to the living room once again.

Kafka, photographed here in 1906, forbade any illustration of a bug from appearing on the cover of his short story "The Metamorphosis." He felt that a visual of a bug could only detract from the situation at hand, the metamorphosis itself. While the bug was an ideal vehicle, Kafka knew instinctively that it could never adequately portray the depth of self-discovery that comes about through transformation.

When he tries to speak to his family, he can make no sound, and the clicking of his jaws frightens them. Thinking that he intends to cause harm, his father tries to drive him back to his room and wounds him with an apple that lodges in his back. Defeated a second time, he retreats to his room, and the door is locked behind him.

Eventually, Grete becomes careless in her duties to Gregor. The family has also taken in three imposing boarders, and Gregor's room is used to store unneeded furniture. Gregor, almost too weak to move, hears violin music coming from the living room. The family, coming to trust him over time, has allowed his door to remain partially open so that he might watch them in the evenings. Overcome by the beauty of Grete's playing and believing that she alone understands and can help him, Gregor enters the family room. Grete is appalled, and the three boarders resolve to leave the house without paying their bill. Defeated a third time, Gregor limps back to his room, where he dies. The family resolves to live more simply in a smaller house in the wake of Gregor's death. Gregor's father assumes his proper role as the primary provider, and his sister blossoms into a beautiful and marriageable woman.

Analysis. Perhaps Kafka's best-known work, "The Metamorphosis" is also his most structured work of fiction. Kafka organized the story into three parts, each featuring an attempt by Gregor to regain his place within the family. In addition, each section focuses on a particular facet of Gregor's life. In the first chapter he considers his transformation in light of its connection to his professional life. In the second he evaluates it in relation to his family life. In the final chapter Gregor must confront his perception of himself.

Kafka compels the reader to engage the story in the first sentence by presenting the literal reality of Gregor's monstrous metamorphosis. As Kafka sustains this bewildering image throughout the story, he denies any metaphorical escape for the reader, who must make sense of an inherently nonsensical proposition, that a man could actually be transformed into an insect. Ironically, Gregor's metamorphosis achieves several goals. It frees him from a job that he detested, it liberates him from the responsibility of being the family provider, and with his eventual death it seems to secure the future happiness of his family.

SOURCES FOR FURTHER STUDY

Citati, Pietro. *Kafka.* New York: Knopf, 1990.

Corngold, Stanley, ed. *The Metamorphosis: Translation Backgrounds and Contexts Criticism.* Norton Critical Edition. New York: Norton and Company, 1996.

Politzer, Heinz. *Franz Kafka: Parable and Paradox.* Ithaca, NY: Cornell University Press, 1966.

Other Works

AMERIKA (1927; English translation, 1938). In *Amerika* Karl Rossmann, a young man banished from his home in Prague in the wake of a scandalous affair with a family maidservant, arrives in New York harbor. Prior to disembarking from the ship, he returns below deck to retrieve his umbrella and loses his way. He meets the ship's stoker, who detains him with a long account of his troubles aboard ship. Sympathizing with the stoker, Karl accompanies him to the ship's captain and intercedes on the stoker's behalf. There Karl meets Edward Jacob, a wealthy senator, who convinces Karl that he is Karl's uncle. Leaving the stoker to an uncertain and ominous fate, Karl accepts his uncle's invitation to live with him, and his future in America seems secure.

Initially overwhelmed by the kindness of his uncle, who provides him with every material and educational need, Karl soon finds life in

C. Schaaf's ca. 1925 image of *#83 Hollandsche Spoor,* the nonstop railway from The Hague to Twenthe in the Netherlands, symbolizes a traveler's search for respite and encapsulates the nonstop cycle of uprootedness that so many of Kafka's characters experience, particularly Karl Rossmann in Kafka's 1927 novel, *Amerika.*

his new home uncomfortably regimented. He accepts an invitation to visit the country estate of Mr. Pollunder, his uncle's business associate. Shortly after his arrival, Karl decides to return, for his uncle had disapproved of the trip. As he prepares to leave, he receives a telegram from his uncle, explaining that Karl can no longer expect any assistance from him and warning Karl not to seek any in the future. Karl leaves Mr. Pollunder's house and walks toward the city.

On the road Karl meets two fellow immigrants, Robinson and Dellamarche, who offer to accompany him to Butterford, where they can all expect to find jobs. Along the way Karl stops at the Hotel Occidental to order food for himself and his two companions. He meets Grete Mitzelbach, the hotel's manageress, who is also from Prague. She invites Karl to stay at the hotel and secures him a job as an elevator operator. Once again, Karl's prospects seem favorable. However, the vast and complicated hierarchy of the hotel overwhelms him, and the head porter eventually dismisses Karl for reasons that are too serious for him to explain.

Back on the road, Karl meets Robinson and Dellamarche, who have improved their circumstances by a connection with a wealthy and overbearing singer, Brunelda. They convince Karl to join them, but he soon finds that their position with the singer is little more than that of a personal servant. He remains with them until he discovers a placard advertising positions with the Nature Theatre of Oklahoma. At a temporary recruiting center, he accepts a position as a "technical worker," and the novel breaks off with Karl on a train, traveling through the vastness of America toward Oklahoma.

It is interesting to note that the German title of this novel is *Der Verschollene*, which translates as "The Man Who Disappeared." Karl Rossman, like the surveyor K., is looking for a secure place and an established identity, having lost his connection to his home in Prague. What he finds in America is a repeating cycle of intimacy and banishment, first with his Uncle Jakob and later in his friendship with Robinson and Delamarche and in his employment at the Hotel Occidental. The unfinished novel leaves Karl on a train, disappearing into the unknown territory of Oklahoma, with only a promise on a placard that the Nature Theatre has a place for everyone.

"IN THE PENAL COLONY" (1919). Written concurrently with *The Trial* in 1914, Kafka's short story "In the Penal Colony" addresses similar issues of guilt, punishment, and the hopelessness of redemption through suffering. On a tropical island, an explorer is invited to witness an execution at the island's penal colony. The officer in charge gives him a thorough and glowing account of the method by which the condemned man will be punished. The apparatus used for executions consists of three parts. The bottom of the machine is a vibrating bed on which the victim is secured. Above the bed hangs the Designer, with its complex array of cogs. In the middle a series of needles, called the Harrow, is arranged in the shape of a human body. The victim is strapped to the bed, and the Designer is set to move the Harrow, which inscribes the broken commandment of the law into his flesh. The process takes 12 hours to complete. The first 6 hours produce unbearable pain, whereas the final 6 produce a calm and redemptive enlightenment just prior to death.

Hoping that the explorer will approve of the device and thereby ensure its continued use, the officer explains that this method of execution has fallen out of favor with the new commandant. He begs the explorer to avoid any response to the execution that could be interpreted as unfavorable. The explorer refuses, and the officer decides to free the condemned man and take his place in the machine, selecting the words *Be Just* to be inscribed on his flesh. As the machine begins its work, it soon malfunctions. The needles of the Harrow impale the officer, and he dies a horrifying death as the instrument of justice disintegrates.

Critics have suggested numerous interpretations of Kafka's rich mixture of symbols within the story. Some stress the opposition between a former, repressive political order, where executions drew large audiences, and the more permissive and humane society, in which the device has fallen out of favor. Others find Kafka's disturbing vision of transfiguration and enlightenment through torture primarily a religious allegory, with the dead commandant always looming on the horizon, as his headstone predicts, like an ominous messiah. Kafka referred to "In the Penal Colony" as his "filthy story." He wrote it during a period of intense personal anguish in 1914, at which time he broke his engagement to Felice Bauer, began work on *The Trial,* and saw the outbreak of the First World War. That the machine kills its victims by writing brings to mind Kafka's own descriptions of his effort to achieve truth in his writing, a process that he often claimed would secure either his salvation or damnation.

"A HUNGER ARTIST" (1924). "A Hunger Artist," written toward the end of Kafka's life, relates the enormous popularity and eventual decline and death of the hunger artist. Renowned for his ability to fast for 40 days, beyond which he was not allowed to go, the hunger artist finds that the public has lost interest in his art. Leaving the service of his manager, he joins a circus, where he hopes to surpass his 40-day record.

The hunger artist occupies a cage near the animal menagerie, and he soon discovers that the crowds of circus goers are more interested in other attractions than in the demonstration of his art, which none seems to understand. As his audience dwindles, so does the care given to his cage. The placards fade, and the board that records the number of fast days achieved is neglected. Neither the public nor the artist himself knows how many days he has fasted. Eventually, attendants, who think that the cage is empty, discover him on the verge of death. He asks their forgiveness and explains that he had hoped to be admired for his fasting, though it was not admirable. "I couldn't find the food I liked. If I had found it, believe me, I should have made no fuss and stuffed myself like you or anyone else."

Kafka uses the image of a professional fast keeper to examine the relationship between an artist and his work and the ability of art to convey meaning to a broader audience. It is during the fast, when he is emaciated and on the verge of death, that the artist feels most alive. It is also that moment when his audience least understands his motives, what he attempts to give them. The hunger artist's art is self-conscious and physically defeating. In contrast, in a cage nearby, the young leopard, unselfconscious and powerful, connects with its audience effortlessly. Ironically, Kafka was correcting the final galleys of a collection of stories, also titled *A Hunger Artist,* when he died. Tuberculosis had spread to his larynx, and it had prevented him from eating or speaking.

Resources

Since 1961, the largest collection of Franz Kafka's original manuscripts has been housed in the Bodleian Library at Oxford University, where they were deposited by Max Brod, with permission from Kafka's heirs. In 1989 an early manuscript of *The Trial* was sold at auction in London for one million pounds and put on exhibit in the German Literary Archives in Marbach, Germany. Since the 1970s an international team of scholars, headed by Malcolm Paisley, has been working on German critical editions of all of Kafka's writings that restore or amend text that was altered by Max Brod.

The first edition, *The Castle,* was published in 1982 by S. Fischer Verlag, and a revised English translation was released in 1998. A proposed second critical edition, to be published in fifteen facsimile volumes by

Stroemfeld Verlag, is also under way. This set will be scanned and reproduced directly from Kafka's handwritten manuscript pages. Other important sources of information on the life and writings of Franz Kafka include the following:

The Kafka Project. Initiated in 1998 by Mauro Nervi, the Kafka Project features a large and growing on-line digital library of Kafka's original manuscripts, letters, and diaries, including scanned images of pages from Kafka's notebooks. The site also contains original translations in several languages, essays on Kafka's life and work from international scholars, and resources for students (http://www.kafka.org).

The Kafka Society of America. Founded in 1975 by Marie Luise Caputo-Mayr of Temple University, the Kafka Society of America meets annually in conjunction with the Modern Language Association of America, to which it is allied, to facilitate scholarly exchange in the field of international Kafka studies. The society also publishes the *Journal of the Kafka Society of America* (http://www.temple.edu/kafka)

PHILIP BADER

Ghassan Kanafani

BORN: April 9, 1936, Acre, Palestine

DIED: July 8, 1972, Beirut, Lebanon

IDENTIFICATION: Twentieth-century Palestinian writer of novels, short stories, literary criticism, and journalism best known for his literary and political dedication to the Palestinian national cause after the 1948 establishment of Israel.

SIGNIFICANCE: Kanafani first achieved wide acclaim for his novel *Rijal fi al-shams* (*Men in the Sun*, 1963), which tells the story of three Palestinian men whose travel in Kuwait in search of employment ends in their death. It was the first artistic work to fully depart from the nostalgia that characterized Palestinian literature after 1948. The tragedy's stark realism and psychological depth startled readers and—when a filmed version was released in 1972—viewers throughout the Arab world. Kanafani remains a famous figure not only for his pioneering fiction and criticism but also for his political activity as a journalist and as a spokesperson for the Popular Front for the Liberation of Palestine.

The Writer's Life

On April 9, 1936, Ghassan Fayiz Kanafani was born in Acre, a northwestern village of orange and olive groves on the Mediterranean coast of then British-controlled Palestine. He was the third child born into the middle-class Muslim family of Muhammad Fayiz 'Abd al-Razzaq Kanafani. Although his mother was illiterate, Kanafani remembered her later in life as a woman of great wisdom and intelligence. His father, Muhammad, a lawyer, was engaged in organized nationalist activity against British occupation and the policy to encourage Zionist immigration at the expense of the local Arab population's welfare. He was imprisoned several times in Kanafani's childhood. When the first Arab-Israeli war arrived in Acre in May 1948, the family left to settle in Damascus, Syria.

Childhood. Born into a turbulent political environment, as a child Kanafani was aware of the national drama unfolding before him. Like many middle-class Arabs of the time, Kanafani was educated in French; he attended a Catholic school in Jaffa until the family left for Damascus.

Palestinians in the same predicament as Kanafani and his family carry bundles of their personal belongings as they flee their homes in 1948, after the outbreak of the Arab-Israeli war. They were brought by truck from a noncombat Arab village near Haifa, in northwest Israel, to this point, where they will take a three-mile hike through no-man's land to Arab lines.

Education in Exile. The Kanafani family's flight left them relatively poor. In Damascus, Kanafani's father established a small law practice, and Kanafani and his brothers helped out by working. Kanafani also studied, completing his high school education in Damascus in 1952. He became an art teacher in a school for Palestinian children who lived, in miserable conditions, in refugee camps. Kanafani, responsible for 1,200 children, expanded his political views when he realized that his students' education must relate to their immediate situation. He began writing short stories, often through the eyes of children, that dramatized the plight of his nation and was introduced to politics by an older Palestinian doctor, George Habash, who would play an influential role in the young writer's life. In 1956 Kanafani followed his sister and brother to Kuwait to teach. Relatively alone in the foreign state, he devoted his time to reading Russian literature and socialist political theory. He began crafting his earlier writing into polished short stories and won a Kuwaiti prize for one.

This photograph of a deserted building and courtyard was taken in Kanafani's homeland of Acre, Palestine, in 1950, just a couple of years after Kanafani and his family fled the city. Kanafani was profoundly influenced by his experiences as a twelve-year-old refugee.

Beirut. In 1960 Kanafani moved to Beirut, the thriving center of Arab intellectual life at the time. The years immediately following his move were busy ones for him, as a writer, as a political thinker, and in his personal life. He ar-

rived in Beirut at the invitation of his mentor, George Habash, to work for the weekly newspaper of the Arab Nationalist Movement, *Hurriya* (Freedom). This group, which believed that all Arab countries should form a united political bloc, was influenced by the promotion of the idea of pan-Arabism by the

HIGHLIGHTS IN KANAFANI'S LIFE

1936   Ghassan Fayiz Kanafani is born on April 9 in Acre, Palestine.
1948   Family flees from war in late spring.
1952   Kanafani graduates from high school in Syria.
1953   Becomes a teacher in refugee camps.
1955   Joins the Arab National Movement; begins publishing short stories.
1956   Travels to Kuwait to teach.
1960   Moves to Lebanon to become a journalist.
1961   Marries Anni Hoover.
1962   *Men in the Sun,* his first novel, is published.
1967   Kanafani becomes spokesman for Popular Front for the Liberation of Palestine and editor of its newspaper, *Al-hadaf.*
1972   Is killed by a car bomb in Beirut, Lebanon, on July 8.

Egyptian president Gamal Abdel Nasser.

In 1961 Kanafani married Anni Hoover, a Danish schoolteacher. Their son, Fayiz, was born in 1962, and four years later, in 1966, their daughter, Lili, was born. In 1962 Kanafana published his first novel, *Men in the Sun,* which brought him renown as a writer.

The Revolutionary Intellectual. In Beirut, Kanafani became an important voice among Palestinian intellectuals. He came to believe that armed struggle was necessary for national liberation. He also believed that a revolution must bring social and economic freedom to all. These ideas were popular throughout the Third World, a bloc of countries that allied themselves neither to the communist Soviet Union nor to the capitalist countries of the West. While he was editor of the newspaper *Al-muharrir* (The Liberator), a post he accepted in

1963, Kanafani traveled to China and India, where he met with political leaders. In 1966 he attended the second Afro-Asian Writers' Conference, in China, where he met other Third World revolutionary authors.

Resistance Literature. In the mid-1960s Kanafani continued to develop his literary technique and his idea that literature and politics could not be separated. The best writers, in his view, promote freedom and express resistance to oppression. His second novel, *Ma tabbaqa lakum (All That's Left to You),* was published in 1966. Notably, unlike Kanafani's first novel about men leaving the land of Palestine, *All That's Left to You* is about a return to the land. In March 1967 Kanafani attended the third Afro-Asian Writers' Conference, in Beirut. There he called attention to Palestinian resistance poets in Israel.

Kanafani in Jordan in 1970. The office he sits in is wallpapered with politically charged posters.

This was a significant event because, since 1948, Palestinian writers in Israel had been isolated from their counterparts in the rest of the Arab world.

After the 1967 War. Kanafani was profoundly affected by the results of the 1967 war. In June 1967 the armies of Egypt and Syria invaded Israel. The invasion was accompanied by much fanfare from President Nasser of Egypt. Israel won the war within days and conquered new territory; the victory revealed the weakness of the Arab governments and armies and especially of Nasser himself. Kanafani turned decisively away from Nasser's pan-Arabism. In October 1967 he became an editor for *Al hadaf* (The Aim), the newspaper of the Popular Front

for the Liberation of Palestine (PFLP). Later he became the Front's spokesman. In 1969 he published his third novel, *'A'id ila Haifa (Returning to Haifa).*

Assassination. As the spokesman for the PFLP, Kanafani was a highly visible political figure connected to a group committed to armed resistance. On July 8, 1972, Kanafani's car blew up when he started it. His 17-year-old niece was with him and also died. It is widely believed that his assassination was carried out by Israeli intelligence agents. His funeral was attended by thousands of people, and his violent death helped confirm him in memory as someone who gave his life for the cause of national liberation.

The Writer's Work

Ghassan Kanafani was a prolific writer. He wrote novellas, short stories, plays, literary criticism, and journalism in a variety of styles. His fiction was generally written in lucid and straightforward prose; his journalism could appear witty and sardonic, as is apparent in a collection of essays he wrote under the pseudonym Faris Faris for the Lebanese newspaper *Al-anwar* in the late 1960s. All of his work is characterized by a passionate commitment to the Palestinian issue and to human freedom.

Politics in Kanafani's Fiction.
Kanafani's fiction is always attuned to the social world and to the micropolitics of human interactions. However, the way he portrayed them changed as his own views developed in the 1950s and 1960s. In his early fiction the world of the Palestinian is often a senseless place, populated by characters who are filled with nostalgia or bitterness over the past. His first novel, *Men in the Sun,* is the culmination of this view. Its main character, Abul Khaizuran, is a bitter former soldier who is so cynical that his only object is to make money, even at the expense of his fellow Palestinians.

The author's increasing commitment to social revolution and armed struggle is reflected in his literature after 1965, a period during which armed incursions into Israel by various guerrilla groups became common. His characters are capable of leaving the past behind without nostalgia and confronting the future as committed revolutionaries. Mother Saad is one such character. In Kanafani's 1969 novel, *Umm Saad,* this mother of a son in a refugee camp encourages her son to become a resistance fighter, even though she knows he may be killed.

George Habash, Kanafani's mentor, is seen here in an undated photograph (right) taken by photographer Nik Wheeler. It was Habash who encouraged Kanafani to take a job with a weekly newspaper in Beirut in 1960. Photographer Roger Wood snapped this photograph (below) of a bustling street scene in Beirut seven years later.

Characters in Kanafani's Fiction.

Kanafani was committed to commemorating the lives and plight of ordinary Palestinians, but this commitment did not mean that his characters would be either innocent or one sided. Rather, everyday people in his works are psychologically complex and often put in situations in which they must make difficult ethical choices. Maryam, in *All That's Left to You,* must face the consequences of her pregnancy by and hasty marriage to a man who betrayed her brother. The Palestinian couple in *Returning to Haifa* must confront the son they had to leave behind in 1948, who has been raised as an Israeli Jew.

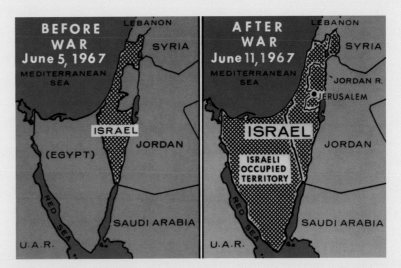

The maps above show the boundaries before and after the six-day war between Arabs and Israelis in June 1967. After it was over, Kanafani quickly lost faith in pan-Arabism and became an editor of and then spokesperson for the Popular Front for the Liberation of Palestine (PFLP).

BIBLIOGRAPHY

Harlow, Barbara. *After Lives: Legacies of Revolutionary Writing.* New York: Verso, 1996.

Kanafani, Anni. *Ghassan Kanafani.* Beirut: Palestine Research Center, 1973.

Siddiq, Muhammad. *Man Is a Cause: Political Consciousness in the Fiction of Ghassan Kanafani.* Seattle: University of Washington Press, 1984.

Wild, Stefan. *Ghassan Kanafani: The Life of a Palestinian.* Wiesbaden: Otto Harrssowitz, 1975.

SOME INSPIRATIONS BEHIND KANAFANI'S WORK

Ghassan Kanafani's outlook was shaped most powerfully by his family's expulsion from their home when he was 12 years old and by his experience of being a refugee. He found sources for his writing in his own childhood memories. Additionally, his work as a teacher in the 1950s was an enduring inspiration to him. He was known for his great affection for children, and many of his short stories are told from the point of view of children, who are both innocent and sharply observant of their surroundings.

Kanafani was also attuned to and influenced by major literary and philosophical trends in the early part of the twentieth century, such as modernism and existentialism. *All That's Left to You,* one of the most successful experiments in Arabic modernism, weaves five characters' streams of consciousness into one narrative in a style that is consciously reminiscent of William Faulkner's *The Sound and the Fury.*

While it is human relationships that are most forcefully portrayed in Kanafani's fiction, his depictions of the desert are also notable. In his works the desert is a stark, unforgiving landscape upon which characters come to terms with their own existence. This view of the desert may have been inspired by Kanafani's lonely years in Kuwait in the late 1950s.

MEN IN THE SUN

Genre: Novel
Published: 1963
Time period: 1958
Setting: Iraq

Themes and Issues. Critics have often seen Kanafani's first novel, about three Palestinian men who die as a consequence of a compatriot's negligence, as an allegory for the failures of Palestinian leaders in the 1948 war. The novel also dramatizes the existential problem of how humans can act in the present to affect their future. Two critics, Benjamin Bennani and Catherine Warner Bennani, have compared Kanafani's novel to the Native American writer Leslie Marmon Silko's *Ceremony*. Both novelists see a virtually spiritual, feminine meaning in the land to which their respective protagonists are connected, and both contain tragic protagonists whose capacity to love has been shaken by historical events.

The Plot. Abu Qais, the first character the reader meets, is an aging farmer who lost his olive grove in the 1948 war. Worried about how he will support his family, he has decided to go to Kuwait. There he hopes he will find work in the lucrative oil industry. When the novel opens, Abu Qais has just arrived in the Iraqi city of Basra and is preparing to find a smuggler who can take him over the Iraq–Kuwait border. Abu Qais soon meets Assad and Marwan, who are also going to Kuwait. Finding someone who will help them make the illegal trip is difficult, however; professional smugglers charge a lot of money, and there is no guarantee they will fulfill their promise. Within a few days the three men meet Abul Khaizuran, a fellow Palestinian who drives a truck that

transports water. Abul Khaizuran had fought in the 1948 war and was surgically castrated when he was injured. Furious at his fate, he has decided that he is interested only in making money, so he agrees to take the men in his truck on his return to Kuwait and charge them less than a professional smuggler.

The scheme he offers Abu Qais, Assad, and Marwan in exchange for his cut-rate deal is dangerous: at both of the two checkpoints on the Iraq–Kuwait border, they will have to hide in the empty metal water tank of his truck. In midday it is so hot that a man cannot survive in it for more than six or seven minutes. Desperate, the men agree to the offer. The first checkpoint is passed without complication. At the second a bored Iraqi official detains Abul Khaizuran and

This desert scene in Oman captures the desolate landscape that Kanafani used as a vehicle to express the plight of his characters, and of real-life Palestinian people, in his first novel, *Men in the Sun*. For Kanafani, the stark, extreme conditions of the desert mirrored the internal isolation felt by generations of Palestinians.

NOVELS

1963 Men in the Sun
1966 All That's Left to You
1969 Returning to Haifa
1969 Umm Saad

SHORT STORY COLLECTIONS

1961 Mawt sarir raqm 12 (The death of bed number twelve)
1962 'Ard al-burtuqal al-hazin (Land of sad oranges)
1965 'Alam laysa lana (A world not for us)
1968 Fi al-rijal wa-al-banadiq (On men and guns)

PLAYS

1964 Al-bab (The door)
1965 Al-jisr 'ila al-'abad (The bridge to forever)

NONFICTION

1967 Fi al-adab al-sihiyuni (On Zionist literature)
1968 Al-adab al-filastini al-maqawim taht al-ihtilal 1948-1968 (Palestinian resistance literature under occupation, 1948–1968)
1972 Thawra 36-39 filastin (Palestine: The 1936–1939 revolt)

GHASSAN KANAFANI

PALESTINE'S CHILDREN

RETURNING TO HAIFA and Other Stories

---

jokes with him, saying that he's been having an affair with a prostitute. Flustered by the impossible story, Abul Khaizuran finally pretends that he has been having the affair. When he runs to the water truck waiting outside, by the time he arrives, the three men have died in the airless tank.

Analysis. The allegorical overtones of *Men in the Sun* were largely achieved through Kanafani's characters. The three men who decide to travel to Kuwait represent a cross section of Palestinian society and are like many men who went looking for work in other countries in the 1950s. The oldest character, the olive farmer Abu Qais, is a typical peasant, deeply attached to his land. Assad goes to Kuwait to make enough money to marry the woman to whom his father has promised him, even though he does not love her, while Marwan, the youngest character, having been abandoned by his father, must find a way to support his family. Their personal dilemmas reflect a society whose circumstances have changed more quickly than its social traditions. The novel startled its readers most, however, because of its portrayal of Abul Khaizuran. Abul Khaizuran's most powerful feelings are humiliation and bitterness. These feelings were widespread among Palestinians after 1948 and reinforced by feelings of failure about having left their land (about half the population was expelled or left out of fear in 1948), but they were not expressed in the literature of the period until Kanafani wrote *Men in the Sun*. Kanafani dramatized Abul Khaizuran's sense that his future does not matter by linking it to his actual failure to have a relationship with a woman or a family of his own. In the last scene of the novel, Abul Khaizuran asks himself why the men did not knock on the walls of the water tank to let him know they were dying. Some critics have understood this to be Kanafani questioning his Palestinian audience about why they were passively accepting their fate instead of actively choosing their future.

SOURCES FOR FURTHER STUDY

Bennani, Benjamin, and Catherine Warner Bennani. "No Ceremony for Men in the Sun: Sexuality, Personhood and Nationhood in Ghassan Kanafani's *Men in the Sun* and Leslie Marmon Silko's *Ceremony*." In *Critical Perspectives on Native American Fiction*, edited by Richard F. Fleck. Washington, DC: Three Continents Press, 1993, pp. 246-255.

Magrath, Douglas R. "A Study of *Rijal Fi al-Shams* by Ghassan Kanafani." *Journal of Arabic Literature* 10 (1979): 95-108.

Other Works

ALL THAT'S LEFT TO YOU (1966). Hamid and Maryam, a brother and sister, have grown up in Gaza (at the southwestern tip of Israel). Their father died when they were young, and they were separated from their mother when they fled from their home city, Jaffa, in 1948. Before he died, their father said that there should be no marriage before the national cause is decided. The novel opens just as Maryam has married Zakaria, because she is carrying his child. Hamid is furious that his sister has brought shame on their family and sets off to find his mother, who lives in Jordan. To get to her, he must pass through the Negev Desert. In the desert he encounters an Israeli soldier, and the two men have a violent confrontation. At the same moment Maryam kills Zakaria, who wants her to abort her baby. *All That's Left to You* is narrated in a stream-of-consciousness style not only by the three human characters but also by the Desert and by Time.

"A HAND IN THE GRAVE" (1962). In this story (published in translation in the same volume as Men in the Sun), Nabil and his classmate Suhail dig up a grave to acquire a skeleton for medical school. When they do, Suhail is sure he has stuck his fingers into the eyes of the corpse. Much later, Nabil learns that the graves were filled with flour sacks, put there by an old peasant for storage. The story puts Kanafani's interest in how the living deal with death in a darkly witty framework; it has a ghostly, gothic quality reminiscent of the stories of Edgar Allen Poe.

Resources

Kanafani's novels and short stories in translation are widely available in libraries and easily purchased at on-line bookstores such as Amazon.com. The 1972 filmed version of *Men in the Sun,* which is titled *Al-makhdu'un (The Duped),* is available in some libraries and is subtitled in English.

The World Wide Web also offers some supplementary information. A biographical essay, with further sources to consult, is available (http://www.kirjasto.sci.fi/kanaf.htm). A thorough review of *All That's Left to You* by Sami Dayal can also be found (http://www.washington-report.org/backissues/0591/9105072).

One can also read the short story "The Land of Sad Oranges," translated by Mona Anis and Hala Halim (http://www.ahram.org.eg/weekly/1998/1948/kanafani.htm).

AMY ZALMAN

Yasunari Kawabata

BORN: June 11, 1899, Osaka, Japan
DIED: April 16, 1972, Zushi, Japan
IDENTIFICATION: Japanese author of lyrical, evocative fiction of loss, longing, beauty, and purity.

SIGNIFICANCE: Kawabata is one of the few Japanese authors to enjoy great critical and popular success both before and after World War II. His first acclaimed work, the short story "Izu no odoriko" ("The Dancing Girl of Izu"; 1926), is still widely read 75 years after its first publication. *Yukiguni* (*Snow Country*; 1948), one of the three novels cited when Kawabata became the first Japanese and second Asian to win the Nobel Prize in literature in 1968, is one of the most celebrated works in Japanese literature. Drawing heavily on classical themes, he is popularly regarded as the most Japanese of twentieth-century authors in his country, but his works also display an acute sense of modernism.

The Writer's Life

Yasunari Kawabata was born on June 11, 1899, in his family home in Osaka. Kawabata's father was a physician, but he died when his son was only two years old. The following year Kawabata's mother also died, and the task of raising the boy was left to his grandparents.

In 1906 Kawabata's grandmother died, and in 1908 his eleven-year-old sister died, and so Kawabata was left alone with his blind grandfather. Kawabata later commented that his tendency to stare at people probably resulted from living with a person who could not see him. Kawabata was 16 years old when his grandfather died. He had no other close relatives to turn to. He later published part of his diary from this period as "Jurokusai no nikki" ("Diary of My Sixteenth Year").

Education and Early Success. Kawabata lived in school dormitories until he entered the prestigious First Higher School in Tokyo. While a student there he made the walking trip down the Izu Peninsula that inspired his most famous short work, "The Dancing Girl of Izu." In 1920 he was admitted to the English literature department of Tokyo University; the following year he transferred to the Japanese literature department, from which he graduated in 1924.

Shortly after graduation Kawabata and several other young writers, including Riichi Yokomitsu, founded a magazine, *Bungei Jidai* (Literary Age), to promote the modernist philosophy of their group, which came to be called the Shinkankakuha, or "new perception" school. However, Kawabata's first major literary success came with the publication in 1926 of a conventional short story, "The Dancing Girl of Izu." In the same year, he wrote the screenplay for *Kurutta ippeiji* (*A Page of Madness*), which was filmed by the modernist director Teinosuke Kinugasa, and also published his first book, *Kanjo soshoku* (*Decorations of the Emotions*), a collection of the first 35 of his so-called palm-of-the-hand stories.

Japan's Izu Peninsula provides the scenic backdrop to Kawabata's acclaimed short story "The Dancing Girl of Izu."

Writer and Critic. Kawabata earned respect as both a writer and literary critic. Although he was often regarded as a solitary figure, one that resembled the detached characters of his literature, Kawabata served on the editorial boards of many major publications, took an active role in the promotion of literature and new writers, wrote reviews, and assumed administrative responsibilities in literary organizations. He was a mentor to many younger writers, including the novelist and playwright Yukio Mishima.

In 1935 Kawabata published the short story "Yugeshiki no kagami" ("Mirror of an Evening Scene") in a magazine. Another related story followed in another magazine, and still another story in a third magazine. In all, Kawabata published eight stories in five magazines; he revised them in 1936 and published them together as the novel *Snow Country,* which was acclaimed as a masterwork. Kawabata added two more stories in 1939 and 1940, so the novel was not in its final form until 1947. The case of *Snow Country* is extreme, but Kawabata's work often evolved from stories he felt he had to develop further after their initial publication.

FILMS BASED ON KAWABATA'S STORIES

1954 *Izu no odoriko (The Dancing Girl of Izu)*

1954 *Yama no oto (The Sound of the Mountain)*

1957 *Yukiguni (Snow Country)*

1967 *Izu no odoriko (The Dancing Girl of Izu)*

1969 *Sembazuru (Thousand Cranes)*

The sixty-nine-year-old Kawabata is toasted by his family and friends at his home near Tokyo after winning the 1968 Nobel Prize in Literature, for which he received $70,000.

HIGHLIGHTS IN KAWABATA'S LIFE

1899	Yasunari Kawabata is born on June 11 in Osaka, Japan.
1901	Kawabata's father dies.
1902	Kawabata's mother dies.
1906	Kawabata's grandmother dies.
1914	Kawabata's grandfather dies.
1918	Kawabata takes a walking tour of Izu Peninsula.
1921	Publishes first story, *"Shokonsai ikkei"* ("A View of Yasukuni Festival").
1924	Graduates from Tokyo University.
1926	Publishes "The Dancing Girl of Izu"; writes screenplay for *A Page of Madness*; publishes first book.
1927	Joins staff of the magazine *Bungakkai* (Literary World).
1935	Publishes first portion of *Snow Country*.
1936	Publishes first novel-length version of *Snow Country*.
1939-1940	Writes two more chapters for *Snow Country*.
1942-1944	Publishes articles on writings of Japanese soldiers killed in action.
1947	Publishes final version of *Snow Country*.
1948	Becomes fourth president of the Japanese PEN Club.
1949	Completes *Thousand Cranes*.
1957	Presides over first International PEN Congress to be held in Japan.
1952	Completes *The Sound of the Mountain*; is awarded literary prize of the Japanese Academy.
1961	Completes *The House of the Sleeping Beauties*; receives the Bunka Kunsho (Order of Cultural Merit), the highest award of the Japanese government.
1961	Publishes *The Old Capital*.
1963	Publishes *Beauty and Sadness*.
1968	Receives Nobel Prize in literature.
1969	Receives honorary doctorate from University of Hawaii.
1970	Travels to Taiwan and Korea.
1972	Dies April 16.

YASUNARI KAWABATA
WINNER OF THE NOBEL PRIZE FOR LITERATURE

BEAUTY AND SADNESS

"Distinguished in purity, supreme clarity of mind, and elegiac tone ... endlessly provocative and original.... A writer of rare intensity."
—*The New York Times Book Review*

Kawabata largely avoided censorship of his work during the war years, which he spent immersing himself in the Japanese classics. What little political content his literature displayed was much too subtle and ambiguous to attract the interest of Japan's militarists.

Kawabata said that after Japan's defeat he could write nothing but elegies, but his writing actually changed little. He became president of the Japanese PEN Club in 1948 and began to travel extensively to develop international understanding of Japanese literature. In the late

1940s and early 1950s, his stature as one of Japan's most critically acclaimed and popular writers was confirmed with such major works as *Thousand Cranes* and *The Sound of the Mountain*, as well as serialized novels such as *Onna de aru koto* (*On Being a Woman*), *Tokyo no hito* (*Tokyo People*), and *Niji ikutabi* (*How Many Rainbows*).

Growing Acclaim. The success of the 1957 International PEN Congress in Tokyo, which Kawabata worked tirelessly to organize, contributed to the rehabilitation of Japan in the eyes of the postwar world and contributed to Kawabata's fame outside Japan. As his administrative responsibilities grew, Kawabata wrote less. His last two novels, *Koto* (*The Old Capital*) and *Utsukushisa to kanashimi* (*Beauty and Sadness*), were published in 1962 and 1963, respectively. Translations of his work into French, German, and English appeared in the 1950s and 1960s, and this attention culminated in Kawabata's becoming the first Japanese writer to be awarded the Nobel Prize in literature, in 1968. The following year, Kawabata was awarded an honorary doctorate by the University of Hawaii, and in 1970 he traveled to Korea and Taiwan.

Kawabata received a great shock in November 1970, when Yukio Mishima killed himself. On April 16, 1972, Kawabata went to his writing studio near the seacoast, and he too apparently committed suicide. His wife and some of his friends believed that it was by accident that he died of gas inhalation. Kawabata left no note.

Kawabata was a mentor to many young writers, including Yukio Mishima, one of Japan's most famous novelists and playwrights. Mishima, an unwavering political activist, seized control of the commanding general's office at a military headquarters near downtown Tokyo, where he is seen speaking to hundreds of Japanese soldiers in November 1970 (above), moments before committing suicide. His suicide stunned Kawabata, who is seated next to Mishima's wife at the Buddhist funeral several weeks later (right).

The Writer's Work

Yasunari Kawabata combined traditional Japanese themes and settings with modern realist fiction and modern writing techniques. He experimented with surrealism and eroticism. His early works were dominated by surrealism and the sensualist school, but his later fiction increasingly incorporated realism back into his stories.

While Kawabata is known for his novels, including *Snow Country* (1948) and *The Sound of the Mountain* (1954), he also wrote more than 140 short tales, which he called "palm-of-the-hand" stories. These were very short, usually only two or three pages long, and many were later collected in anthologies by both Kawabata and others. Kawabata wrote a number of screenplays, tales, and essays that formed the basis for his later novels (for instance, *Snow Country* is really a collection of eight previously published tales).

Russian artist Irina Ilina's *Dreams about Japan* reflects the surrealism and eroticism that embody Kawabata's earlier work.

Themes in Kawabata's Fiction.
Many of Kawabata's works have a sexual theme and explore the place and role of sex in modern society and culture. Hence, Kawabata often used his characters to portray traditional components of Japanese culture, including devotion to family, in a rapidly evolving society that often downplayed or discarded these ideals. Concurrently, many of his works revolve around complicated sexual plots; for example, *Beauty and Sadness* (1963) is based on a revenge motif. Like many authors, Kawabata incorporated experiences from his own life in his work. "The Dancing Girl of Izu" is partially based on Kawabata's own infatuation with a dancer in his youth, and Komako, the geisha from *Snow Country,* is modeled after a real woman the author knew.

Characters in Kawabata's Fiction.
In *The Sound of the Mountain,* Kawabata's central character is Shingo. Like many of the writer's main characters, Shingo represents the traditional Japanese em-

SOME INSPIRATIONS BEHIND KAWABATA'S WORK

Despite the fact that he was a twentieth-century author, much of Yasunari Kawabata's work draws upon traditional Japanese themes or is inspired by Japan's culture. For instance, *The Master of Go* (1969) not only revolves around the ancient Japanese game of go but is set during a fictional match between an old master and a rising star in 1938. Furthermore, Kawabata studied the Japanese classics, such as *The Tale of Genji* from the eleventh century, as well as Buddhist scriptures, the Bible, and Western classics, and these older influences surface in a number of his works, such as *The Sound of the Mountain*. Kawabata was drawn to the literary innovations of the early twentieth century as well. He experimented with styles and themes inspired by avant-garde European writers, and his admiration of the work of these modernists manifested itself in many of his works, most notably in his *Palm-of-the-Hand Stories*.

An example of Kawabata's utilization of Japanese culture, the Japanese game of go is used as an organizing device in Kawabata's novel *The Master of Go*. This photograph, taken around 1900, shows two actors—one portraying a *daimyo*, or a feudal lord, and the other a Shinto priest—playing a game of go.

phasis on family, even though his family is dysfunctional on a variety of levels and Shingo's actions often exacerbate the family's problems. As the family faces a succession of crises, Kawabata portrays Shingo in a sympathetic and warm fashion in spite of his flaws.

While Shingo represents Kawabata's realist facet, Shimamura from *Snow Country* exemplifies the author's surrealist inclinations. Shimamura is incapable of living life to its fullest and survives only as an observer, not as a participant. Instead of living in the real world, Shimamura becomes absorbed or swept into a netherworld. He therefore misses any opportunities for true love or happiness.

BIBLIOGRAPHY

Akiyama, Masayuki. *A Comparative Study of Henry James and Major Japanese Writers*. Tokyo: Nan'un-Do, 1991.

Gessel, Van C. *Three Modern Novelists: Soseki, Tanizaki, Kawabata*. New York: Kodansha International, 1993.

Janeira, Armando Martins. *Japanese and Western Literature*. Rutland, VT: Charles E. Tuttle, 1970.

Keene, Donald. *Dawn to the West*. New York: Holt, Rinehart and Winston, 1984.

Kimball, Arthur G. *Crisis in Identity*. Rutland, VT: Charles E. Tuttle, 1973.

Lewell, John. *Modern Japanese Novelists*. New York: Kodansha International, 1993.

Lippit, Noriko Mizuta. *Reality and Fiction in Modern Japanese Literature*. White Plains, NY: Sharpe, 1980.

Petersen, Gwenn Broadman. *The Moon in the Water: Understanding Tanizaki, Kawabata, and Mishima*. Honolulu: University of Hawaii Press, 1979.

Pollack, David. *Reading against Culture: Ideology and Narrative in the Japanese Novel*. Ithaca, NY: Cornell University Press, 1992.

Swann, Thomas E., and Kinya Tsuruta, eds. *Approaches to the Modern Japanese Short Story*. Tokyo: Waseda University Press, 1982.

Starrs, Roy. *Soundings in Time: The Fictive Art of Kawabata Yasunari*. Richmond, UK: Japan Library, 1998.

"THE DANCING GIRL OF IZU"

Genre: Short story
Published: Tokyo, 1925
Time period: Early 1920s
Setting: Izu Peninsula, southwest of Tokyo

Themes and Issues. Kawabata's most famous short story and his first work introduced the theme of yearning for the virginal and ultimately unattainable beauty that was to become a recurring feature in his literature. The story also touches on social questions of class difference, though Kawabata addressed such issues seldom and in his later works only obliquely. The story also raises the question of self-worth, a common theme in many of Kawabata's more autobiographical works.

The Plot. A student on holiday from a prestigious school takes a solitary walking trip down the Izu Peninsula. He is attracted to a girl he meets among a troupe of itinerant performers; he wonders, given the reputation of such low-class performers, how he might arrange to sleep with her. Later, when he happens to catch sight of her naked at a public bath, the student realizes that the girl is much younger than her hair style and makeup had made her appear and thus is too young for sex. Still, the student continues to travel with the troupe, though the performers insist that the wealthier student not stay in the cheap lodging houses with them. As they travel, the student, whose own doubts and self-loathing had made him feel others could not love him, realizes, through the kindness of the performers and through the trust that other strangers seem willing to extend him, that he may indeed be the "nice person" that others see. He returns to Tokyo by boat, having parted from the entertainers and feeling a sweet but melancholy sense of healing.

Analysis. "Dancing Girl" introduced the yearning for virginal beauty that would recur throughout Kawabata's work. Far from being disappointed with the discovery of the girl's unavailability, the student is instead released from the anxiety that had accompanied his sexual quest. The dancing girl remains distant and pure. The student, too, feels purified and affirmed by his encounter with these people, who come from a world so different from his.

The longing for pure and unattainable beauty, illuminated by a student's desire for a troupe dancer in the short story "The Dancing Girl of Izu," is a hallmark theme in Kawabata's writing.

LONG FICTION

1948 Snow Country
1952 Thousand Cranes
1954 The Sound of the Mountain
1954 The Lake
1957 On Being a Woman
1961 The Old Capital
1963 Beauty and Sadness
1972 The Master of Go

SHORT STORIES AND COLLECTIONS

1926 "The Dancing Girl of Izu"; Decorations of the Emotions
1933 Of Birds and Beasts

1935 "Mirror of an Evening Scene"
1955 Tokyo People; How Many Rainbows
1958 First Snow on Fuji
1961 The House of the Sleeping Beauties and Other Stories
1964 One Arm
1988 Palm-of-the-Hand Stories (posthumous trans. by Lane Dunlop and J. Martin Holman of 70 of Kawabata's short stories)

NONFICTION

1969 The Existence and Discovery of Beauty; Japan the Beautiful and Myself

---

SNOW COUNTRY

Genre: Novel
Published: Tokyo, 1935–1947
Time period: 1930s
Setting: The "snow country" along the northern coast of Japan's main island, Honshu

Themes and Issues. Throughout *Snow Country* Kawabata develops his characters so that there are significant distances between them. These gulfs exist on both the physical level, in terms of geographic distance, and the emotional level. This way of working allowed the author to underline the fear of intimacy and closeness that infuses his characters and to highlight the potential problems caused by their inability to open themselves. Even the most promising of relationships are doomed to fail because of the rigidity of people who reflect the constraints of Japanese society of the time. Kawabata also uses this technique to highlight the dichotomy of Japanese culture, where people are able to develop deep attachments to nature but are unable to form similar bonds with their fellow humans.

The Plot. A Tokyo dilettante, Shimamura, makes a late-autumn train trip to a region known for its hot springs and heavy snows. Komako, a geisha with whom he had had a relationship on a previous visit, visits his room often. Though she loves him, Shimamura is incapable of love. Shimamura is drawn to the young woman Yoko, who cares for a sickly man, whose relationship to her is a mystery. Shimamura is merely an observer, however, not a participant. In the end, Shimamura watches as Komako carries Yoko away from a burning building from which the young woman has leaped. The novel concludes with Shimamura looking up at the Milky Way, which seems to flow into him.

Analysis. Shimamura's travels to the "snow country," away from his family and daily life in Tokyo, mark his entrance into a netherworld. The train window, which acts as an imperfect mirror, suggests, however, the separation this man will still feel even as he experiences the suggestive sensuousness of this world. The evocative landscape plays a major role in the lyricism of the novel, as do the landscapes in many of Kawabata's other works. In the end Kawabata's characters, rarely drawn to each other, seem to merge instead with nature.

Other Works

PALM-OF-THE-HAND STORIES (1923–1972). Throughout his career Kawabata wrote more than 140 very short stories, each averaging about two pages in length. Although these stories are diverse in content and theme and share no recurring characters (except the first-person narrator who resembles Kawabata, at least as he depicts himself in the few autobiographical stories), Kawabata considered them to form a group.

Many critics regard the short story as Kawabata's basic unit of literary construction, the core construct from which he fashioned his longer works. Each story's shortness makes its effectiveness dependent on either an image that encapsulates the essence of a theme or a bit of dialogue that reveals much despite its brevity. Kawabata's loyalty to this form is shown by the fact that his last published work was a "palm-sized" distillation of his most famous novel, *Snow Country*.

THE SOUND OF THE MOUNTAIN (1954). Shingo, haunted by memories and longings he cannot grasp or fulfill, is troubled by the first signs of senility. Having been in love with his wife's late sister and now drawn to his own daughter-in-law, he feels premonitions of death, even as he observes in his own family the curious form that new birth has taken: his daughter-in-law aborts her unfaithful husband's baby, and her husband's former mistress decides to give birth even after she has severed relations with Shingo's son. The sympathy and warmth with which Kawabata depicts his characters and evokes familiar themes make *The Sound of the Mountain* particularly poetic and moving.

Resources

There are a number of English-language resources on Kawabata readily available on the Web, including the following:

Books and Writers. This Web site features a biography, a bibliography, and links, as well as excerpts from Kawabata's writing (http://www.kirjasto.sci.fi/kawabata.htm).

Nobel E-Museum. The Nobel Society maintains a Web site that has information on Kawabata, including a biography, Kawabata's Nobel lecture from 1968, and links to resources (http://www.nobel.se/literature/laureates/1968/).

Yasunari Kawabata Bibliography. This Web site evolved out of a school project and contains an exhaustive list of material about the author and his works. Each of the entries is annotated with a short description of the work (http://www.otterbein.edu/home/fac/plarchr/kawabata.htm).

MARTIN HOLMAN

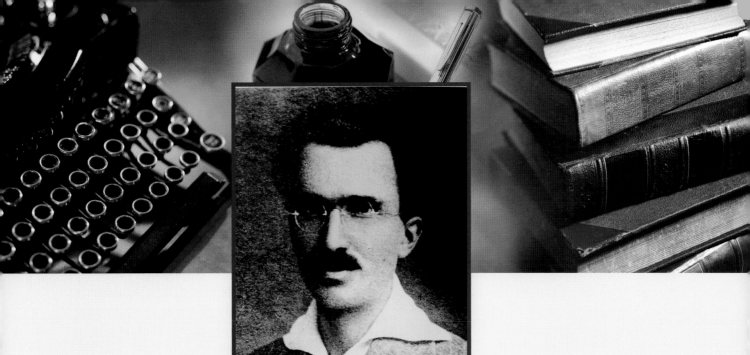

Nikos Kazantzakis

BORN: February 18, 1883, Iráklion, Crete (Greece)
DIED: October 26, 1957, Freiburg, West Germany
IDENTIFICATION: Mid-twentieth-century Cretan novelist, poet, travel writer, dramatist, essayist, and philosopher best known for his socially controversial works, several of which have been made into important films.

SIGNIFICANCE: Among the most popular authors of the twentieth century, Kazantzakis was a prolific professional writer and intellectual working within a broad range of genres. Outside Greece, Kazantzakis is best known for his novels and his epic poem, *Odissia (The Odyssey: A Modern Sequel),* a work he considered his most crucial. In addition to this poem, his international stature is largely due to novels published in the last decade of his life, including *Vios ke politia tu Aléksi Zorbá (Zorba the Greek)* and *O teleftaíos pirasmós (The Last Temptation of Christ).* Narrowly denied the Nobel Prize but translated into forty-nine languages, he remains the best-known modern Greek author to international audiences.

On February 18, 1883, Nikos Kazantzakis was born in Iráklion, the capital of Crete. The island was still in the grip of Ottoman control, and he witnessed repeated revolts against Turkish rule. A firstborn and only surviving son, he had two younger sisters, Anastasía (b. 1884) and Eléni (b. 1887), and a younger brother, Giorgos (b. 1890), who died in infancy. His father, Míhalis, a formidable and respected man, was a farmer and merchant. His mother, María Christodouláki, came from a peasant family. Although he was to travel widely throughout his life and spend his last years in exile, the land of Crete and its people and their language and their struggle for liberty remained a constant source of inspiration.

Formative Years: Family and Crete.
Nikos's father was a dark and dominating figure. A man of action, he participated in the rebellion of 1898. Nikos feared he would never measure up to his father's expectation that he be a *pallikári,* an intrepid lover of freedom, who would bring honor to his name. Nikos viewed his mother as a saint. In his semiautobiography, *Anaforá stan Gréko (Report to Greco),* Kazantzakis recounts a searing story from his childhood. One night as the Turks of Iráklion massacred Greeks in the town, his father bolted the door and sharpened his knife, swearing he would cut the throats of his family before allowing them to be taken. Next morning, father and son went to the harbor, where they found the bodies of Christians hanged in the square. His father made him kiss these martyrs' feet to remember the price of liberty. Although terrified, Kazantzakis later understood his father was trying to imbue in him the code of the *pallikária.*

Education. The family fled to the island of Naxos in 1897, and his father returned to help liberate Crete. Nikos enrolled in the French Franciscan School, where he was introduced to Western ideas, learned French and Italian, and excelled in his studies. Clearly Kazantzakis's future path lay in the struggles of the mind, a fact that his father came to acknowledge.

Returning to Crete and graduating from high school, he studied law and completed his degree

Kazantzakis's controlling father, Míhalis, as he appeared in 1883, the year Kazantzakis was born. More than a half a century later, Kazantzakis would model his character Kapetán Mihális, the ultimate *pallikári* (a fearless lover of freedom), after his father in his 1953 novel, *Freedom or Death.*

(1902–1906) at the University of Athens. There Kazantzakis began his literary career with the publication of a novella, *Ofis ke kríno (Serpent and Lily)*, in 1906 and his first play, *Ksimeróne (Day is Breaking)*, which was produced the following year and won a prize amid controversy.

Kazantzakis moved to Paris and studied with the French philosopher Henri Bergson. He was imbued with the vitalism of Bergson and the nihilism of the German philosopher Friedrich Nietzsche. These two thinkers deeply influenced Kazantzakis's philosophy. Bergson offered the belief that an *élan vital,* or life force, transubstantiates flesh into spirit, and Nietzsche offered the concept of the superman who transforms himself by will. Kazantzakis lost faith, agreeing with his hero Nietzsche that "God is dead!" He wrote his dissertation (1909) on Nietzsche at Athens.

Kazantzakis the Nationalist.

Returning to Crete, Kazantzakis became involved in the movement to adopt the demotic language (the speech of the common people) as the official language of the state in place of Katharevusa (a modern form of classical Greek). Believing that Greek national literature must be expressed in the people's language, Kazantzakis used the demotic in his writings.

An ardent supporter of the Greek statesman Eleuthérios Venizélos's Great Idea, the belief that Constantinople and the lands of ancient Greece should be liberated from the Turkish yoke and unified in a Greek state, Kazantzakis served in Venizélos's office. Possibly to avoid military service, he also engaged in commercial ventures from 1915 to 1917, working with Giorgos Zorbás, the inspiration for his novel *Zorba the Greek.*

Kazantzakis was appointed director general of the Ministry of Welfare

Kazantzakis in his hometown of Iráklion, the capital of the island of Crete, in 1905 with his mother (seated) and his two sisters, Anastasía (left) and Eléni. Being the only surviving son, there was great pressure on Kazantzakis to bring honor to the family name.

in 1919, charged with the repatriation of 150,000 ethnic Greeks being persecuted in the Caucasus. These events provided the basis for his novel *O Hristós ksanastavrónetai (The Greek Passion)*. After the political defeat of Venizélos in 1920, Kazantzakis resigned. With Greece's defeat in 1922, Kazantzakis became disillusioned with chauvinistic nationalism.

Kazantzakis the Internationalist. Kazantzakis lived in Vienna and Berlin from 1922 to 1924. In Vienna he studied Buddhism and began writing his play *Vúdas (Buddha)*. Moving to Berlin, he lived among a circle of young Jewish radicals. Drawn to a new superman, Lenin, he abandoned nationalism for international communism. He wrote *Salvatores Dei: Askitikí (The Saviors of God: Spiritual Exercises)*, a lyrical attempt to explicate his credo; it was modeled on Saint Ignatius Loyola's *Spiritual Exercises*.

In Greece in 1924, Kazantzakis met Eléni Samíou. In 1925 he was briefly arrested in Iráklion for communist activity and traveled to the Soviet Union as a correspondent. In 1926 he divorced Galatea, whom he had married in 1911, to live with Eléni and continued his travels as a correspondent in Palestine, Cyprus, Spain, and Italy. In 1927 he continued this work in Egypt and Sinai, returning to Russia as a guest of the government. Kazantzakis eventually became disillusioned and wrote the novel *Toda-Raba (Moscou a crié)* in 1929 in French as commentary on Soviet communism.

Depression and War. By the 1930s Kazantzakis was committed to the life of a professional writer. In this decade he established his first permanent residence, in 1936, on the Greek island of Aegina. He translated, wrote textbooks, and worked on his epic poem, *Odyssey*, which was finally published in 1938. He traveled in Spain in 1932 and 1933 and in Japan and China in 1935. He wrote another novel in French based on his Far Eastern travels, *Le jardin des rochers (The Rock Garden*, 1936), and traveled to Spain to cover the Spanish civil war, interviewing the Spanish Nationalist leader Francisco Franco and the philosopher Miguel de Unamuno. His accounts of journeys in the Morea and Spain were published the next year. In 1939 he visited England and published his account of that journey in 1941. Kazantzakis's travel accounts earned him well-deserved admiration (some critics claim they are his best work) and supported his journeying.

He spent the war years on Aegina writing feverishly, composing his trib-

This photograph of Kazantzakis was taken in 1912 while he was a volunteer soldier during the First Balkan War, in which Greece, along with Bulgaria, Serbia, and Montenegro, was successful in seizing Macedonia from Turkey.

HIGHLIGHTS IN KAZANTZAKIS'S LIFE

1883	Nikos Kazantzakis is born on February 18 in Iráklion, Crete.
1902	Graduates from the gymnasium in Iráklion.
1902–1906	Completes law degree in Athens.
1907–1909	Studies philosophy in Paris.
1909	Completes dissertation on Nietzsche.
1911	Marries Galatea Alexíou.
1917	Mines lignite with Giorgos Zorbás.
1919	Directs rescue mission in Caucasus.
1922–1924	Lives in Vienna and Berlin.
1926	Divorces Galatea.
1926–1929	Is correspondent in Spain, Italy, Palestine, Cyprus, Egypt, and Russia.
1929–1930	While in Czechoslovakia writes novels in French; moves to France.
1932–1933	Moves to Spain; returns to Greek island of Aegina.
1935	Travels to Japan and China.
1938	Publishes *The Odyssey.*
1939	Travels to England.
1940–1944	Returns to Aegina during World War II; writes productively.
1945	Marries Eléni Samíou; is appointed minister of national education.
1946	Resigns government post; is nominated for the Nobel Prize; begins political exile.
1947	Is appointed director of UNESCO Bureau of Translations.
1948	Resigns UNESCO position; settles in Antibes, France.
1949	Novels achieve success in translation.
1953	Greek Orthodox Church attempts to prosecute Kazantzakis for blasphemy in *The Last Temptation of Christ.*
1954	Kazantzakis is diagnosed with leukemia; Vatican bans *The Last Temptation of Christ.*
1955	After royal intervention *The Last Temptation* is published in Greece.
1956	Kazantzakis is awarded the Lenin Peace Prize but loses Nobel Prize vote.
1957	Visits China; dies on October 26 in Freiburg, West Germany, and is buried in Iráklion.

Kazantzakis's widely attended funeral ceremony at the Cathedral of St. Minas in Iráklion on November 5, 1957 (left), and a photograph, taken on the same day, of his grave in the Venetian ramparts along the city wall of Iráklion.

ute to Zorbás (1941–1943) and the dramas *Buddha, Promithéas* (Prometheus), *O Kapodístrias* (Capodistria), and *Konstandinos o Palaiológos* (Constantine Palaiologos) and translating the *Iliad.* In 1945 he returned to politics, married Eléni, and joined the coalition government as minister of education. The following year he resigned his post, and as civil war erupted, he began a political exile, first in England and then in France, that continued until his death.

Last Years. In 1947 Kazantzakis accepted a post with UNESCO for a year. After resigning, he settled with Eléni in Antibes, France, and a productive period began, in which he wrote his most successful novels. In these years Kazantzakis experienced a meteoric rise in his international reputation. *Zorba* was published in France in 1947; he drafted *The Greek Passion,* which was published in Swedish in 1950; and in 1951 he completed a draft of *The Last Temptation of Christ.*

By 1952 Kazantzakis was published throughout Europe except in Greece. He published *O Kapetán Mihális (Freedom or Death)* in 1953 and wrote *St. Francis.* The Greek Orthodox Church took great offense to parts of *Freedom or Death* and the entire *Last Temptation,*

although the latter had not been published in Greek, and sought to prosecute him for sacrilege.

In 1953 Kazantzakis's health failed, and a lingering eye infection caused the loss of an eye. A diagnosis of benign lymphatic leukemia in 1954 explained his lifelong bouts with facial eczema. In the same year *The Last Temptation of Christ* was placed on the Roman Catholic Index of Forbidden Books. In 1955 he consulted with the director Jules Dassin on a screenplay for *The Greek Passion,* the first film version of his work (the film was released in 1957). *The Last Temptation* was finally published in Greece in 1955, after King Paul himself intervened on its behalf.

In 1956 Kazantzakis received the Lenin Peace Prize in Vienna and lost the Nobel Prize by one vote. After visiting the People's Republic of China as a guest of the government, he died in Freiburg, West Germany, from complications of an infected vaccination and influenza on October 26, 1957. When his body arrived in Athens, church authorities refused to allow it to lie in state. His funeral in Iráklion was widely attended, and he was interred in the Venetian ramparts. His epitaph summarizes his philosophy: "I hope for nothing. I fear nothing. I am free."

The Writer's Work

Nikos Kazantzakis was, in his own phrase, a "quill driver." He was a wanderer and searcher, both physically and spiritually, much like his hero Odysseus. During a span of more than 60 years, he wrote novels, plays, travel commentary, poetry, essays, letters, philosophy, journalism, children's literature and textbooks, memoirs, autobiographical fiction, numerous translations, and encyclopedia articles, as well as keeping up a voluminous correspondence.

Themes in Kazantzakis's Fiction.

Kazantzakis's great theme is the metaphor that he called the "Cretan glance." He recognized it in the frescoes of ancestral bullfighters on the walls of the Minoan palace of Knossos. He saw it in the flinty eyes of the *pallikária* of Crete in their resistance against overwhelming odds. It is the capacity of man, "without hope yet without fear," to experience life to the fullest while facing the abyss. This quality dignifies the individual human. All Kazantzakis's heroes display this quality.

Another facet of this theme is drawn from Kazantzakis's philosophical work, *The Saviors of God: Spiritual Exercises.* It is only through individual dialectical struggle that the long, hard ascent of man from flesh transubstantiated to spirit may be achieved. Through this process the individual man saves God. It was for this heretical but ultimately positive religious view that Kazantzakis, the atheist, was denounced. This dialectical struggle is a consistent theme in all his works.

People in Kazantzakis's Fiction.

The novels are often semiautobiographical, but rather than play the major role, Kazantzakis's voice is frequently that of a subordinate character, such as Brother Leo in *O ftohúlis tou Théu (St. Francis),* who serves as both narrator and supporter of the hero of the story.

The heroes of Kazantzakis's tales are supermen—*übermenschen,* in Nietzschian terms. Called colossi by Kazantzakis, these men in-

Artist Georg I. Regierungszeit's woodcut depiction of the massacre of Turkish soldiers by Christian Cretans, which appeared in the July 1896 publication of *Petit Journal,* illustrates one of Kazantzakis's great themes, the "Cretan glance," described as the ability of mankind to act "without hope yet without fear."

SOME INSPIRATIONS BEHIND KAZANTZAKIS'S WORK

Nikos Kazantzakis drew his inspiration from a variety of sources. As a child growing up in Crete, he was immersed in a rich oral tradition. He was raised on the traditional stories of the heroes of the Cretan resistance, as well as on folktales and the legends of the Christian saints. As a small boy Nikos voraciously read aloud the popular lives of the saints, embellishing them and passing them off as his own adventures in tales he spun for his playmates. He credited this process as his introduction to creative writing.

Although he would spend most of his life wandering elsewhere, Crete and its people were his principal inspirations. Many of the people he remembered from his youth appear as characters in his literary inventions. He also felt the heavy influence of his ancestors, as well as the domineering figure of his father, the model for Kapetán Mihális, the hero of his novel *Freedom or Death.* Believing that he had both Jewish and Arab blood in his veins, along with that of his Christian ancestors, he saw both Crete and himself as poised between East and West. In this sense he felt that Cretan particulars could express universal meaning.

Many other people and experiences influenced his writing, but perhaps the greatest of these was the man he called his great mentor, Giorgos Zorbás, who provided the model for the title character of *Zorba the Greek.*

Finally, the towering figures of philosophy, religion, art, and literature, including especially Friedrich Nietzsche, Henri Bergson, Christ, Buddha, Dante, Homer (specifically, Odysseus), El Greco, and Lenin, permeate his work. Kazantzakis absorbed the canon of Western literature and culture but, as did his mentor El Greco, transformed this influence through the prism of Crete.

The charismatic and loveable rogue Zorba in Kazantzakis's best-known work, *Zorba the Greek,* was crafted from Kazantzakis's real-life comrade and mentor Giorgos Zorbás, seen here in 1918.

clude Manolios in *The Greek Passion,* Zorba, and Christ; they are men who can face death while taking action without hope or fear. Based on the Cretan ideal of the *pallikári,* these men often fail to attain their goals but are reborn again in spirit because they turn their back on mundane pleasure through sheer exertion of will.

Kazantzakis's heroes are men. Women invariably are portrayed as dangerous or superficial, and although desirable for reproduction, ultimately they are obstacles to the heroic male's ascent to the transubstantiation of flesh to spirit. Thus, Christ must reject the temptation of his lust for Magdalene and the comforts of domesticity; the shepherd Manolios of *The Greek Passion* must renounce his carnal love for Lenio. Kapetán Mihális and Nuri Bey in *Freedom or Death* find their brotherhood dashed by their common lust for Eminé, and in *The Fratricides* the former comrades Drakos and the captain find their hatred accentuated by the sexual and political betrayal of the captain's wife.

This view, which many would term sexist, finds some of its roots in the values of the Cretan *pallikária*, to which Kazantzakis makes his heroes adhere. As the biographer Peter Bien has observed, it remains one of the great limitations upon his art.

Kazantzakis's Literary Legacy. Almost half a century after Kazantzakis's death in 1957, his place in world literature remains undetermined. Yet he remains the best-known and most controversial Greek writer of the twentieth century. As it did during his life, his work continues to engender reactions at the extremes. In Greece he is still either loathed or venerated. Some contemporary critics have dismissed his work as poorly crafted, egotistic, misogynist, and inconsequential. In contrast, Morton P. Levitt and Kimon Friar consider him among the great modernists of the twentieth century, in company with James Joyce, Thomas Mann, D. H. Lawrence, Franz Kafka, and Marcel Proust.

In the United States and Europe it is Kazantzakis's novels that remain most popular, especially *Zorba the Greek* and *The Last Temptation of Christ*. The group of novels published in the last decade of his life coupled with his epic poem, *The Odyssey: A Modern Sequel*, established his place with an international audience. Peter Bien has argued that much of this popularity resulted from the inherent romanti-

cism and exoticism of his novels and their message that "a vision of life that included irrationalism could still be positive."

In recent years Kazantzakis's conceptions of God and his philosophical struggles in and through his art have become an important focus of academic philosophical and religious discussion. This recognition would have pleased a man who saw his art as a vehicle through which humans could become "saviors of God."

BIBLIOGRAPHY

Bien, Peter. *Kazantzakis: Politics of the Spirit.* Princeton, NJ: Princeton University Press, 1989.

—-. *Kazantzakis and the Linguistic Revolution in Greek Literature.* Princeton, NJ: Princeton University Press, 1972.

—-. *Nikos Kazantzakis.* New York: Columbia University Press, 1972.

—-. *Nikos Kazantzakis: Novelist. Studies in Modern Greek.* New Rochelle, NY: Aristide D. Caratzas, 1989.

—-. *Tempted by Happiness: Kazantzakis' Post-Christian Christ.* Wallingford, PA: Pendle Hill Publications, 1984.

Dombrowski, Daniel A. *Kazantzakis and God.* Albany: State University of New York Press, 1997.

Durant, Will, and Ariel Durant. *Interpretations of Life: A Survey of Contemporary Literature,* Ch. 16, "Kazantzakis." New York: Simon and Schuster, 1970.

Kazantzakis, Helen. *Nikos Kazantzakis: A Biography Based on His Letters.* New York: Simon and Schuster, 1968.

Lea, James F. *Kazantzakis: The Politics of Salvation.* Tuscaloosa: University of Alabama Press, 1979.

Levitt, Morton P. *The Cretan Glance: The World and Art of Nikos Kazantzakis.* Columbus: Ohio State University Press, 1980.

Middleton, Darren J. N. *Novel Theology: Nikos Kazantzakis's Encounter with Whiteheadian Process Theism.* Macon, GA: Mercer University Press, 2000.

Middleton, Darren J. N., and Peter Bien, eds. *God's Struggler: Religion in the Writings of Nikos Kazantzakis.* Macon, GA: Mercer University Press, 1996.

Poland, Larry W. *The Last Temptation of Hollywood.* Highland, CA: Mastermedia International, 1988.

Prevelakis, Pantelis. *Nikos Kazantzakis and His Odyssey: A Study of the Poet and the Poem.* New York: Simon and Schuster, 1961.

NOVELS

1906   Ofis ke kríno (Serpent and Lily, translated 1980)

1909   Spasménes psihés (Broken souls)

1934   Toda-Raba: Moscou a Crié (Toda Raba, 1964)

1936   Le jardin des rochers (The Rock Garden, 1963)

1946   Víos ke politía tu Aléksi Zorbá (Zorba the Greek, 1952)

1953   O Kapetán Mihális (Freedom or Death, 1956)

1954   O Hristós ksanas-tavrónetai (The Greek Passion, 1954; the more literal British title is Christ Re-crucified, 1954)

1955   O teleftaíos pirasmós (The Last Temptation of Christ, 1960)

1956   O ftohúlis tou Theú (St. Francis, 1962; British title: God's Pauper: St. Francis of Assisi, 1962)

1963   I aderfofádes (The Fratricides, 1964)

CHILDREN'S LITERATURE

1979   Mégas Aléxandros (Alexander the Great, 1982)

1981   Sta palátia tís knosóu (At the Palaces of Knossos, 1988)

PLAYS

1907   Ksimerónei (Day Is Breaking)

1909   Komodía (Comedy, 1975)

1910   O protomástoras (The master builder)

1927   Nikifóros Fokás (Nikiforos Fokas)

1928   Hristós (Christ)

1928   Odisséas (Odysseus)

1939   Mélissa (Melissa, 1969)

1945   Iulianós o paravátis (Julian the apostate)

1946   O Kapodístrias (Capodistria)

1955   Kúros (Kouros, 1969)

1955   Promithéas (Prometheus)

1956   Hristóforos Kolómvos (Christopher Columbus, 1969)

1956   Konstandínos o Palaiológos (Constantine Palaiologos)

1956   Sódoma ke Gómora (Sodom and Gomorrah, 1982)

1956   Vúdas (Buddha, 1983)

1962   O Othéllos ksanayirízei (Othello returns)

POETRY

1938   Odíssia (The Odyssey: A Modern Sequel, 1958)

1960   Tertsínes (Terzinas)

TRAVELS

1928   Tí eída sti Rusía (Russia: A Chronicle of Three Journeys in the Aftermath of the Revolution, 1989)

1937   O Moreás (Journey to the Morea, 1965)

1937   Taksidévondas: Ispanía (Spain, 1963)

1938   Iaponía-Kína (Japan, China: A Journal of Two Voyages to the Far East, 1935 and 1957, 1963)

1941   Taksidévondas: Anglia (England: A Travel Journal, 1965)

1961   Taksidévondas (Journeying: Travels in Italy, Egypt, Sinai, Jerusalem and Cyprus, 1975)

ESSAYS

1906   "I arrósteia tu aiónos" ("The Sickness of the Century," In Serpent and Lily, 1980)

1927   Salvatores Dei. Askitikí (The Saviors of God: Spiritual Exercises, 1960)

1954   "To drama ke o simerínos ánthropos" ("Drama and Contemporary Man," 1976)

1971   Simposíon (Symposium, 1974)

AUTOBIOGRAPHY

1961   Anaforá ston Gréko (Report to Greco, 1965)

CORRESPONDENCE

1958   Epistolés pros ti Galatía (The Suffering God: Selected Letters to Galatia and to Papastephanou, 1979)

Reader's Guide to Major Works

ZORBA THE GREEK

Genre: Novel
Subgenre: Picaresque tragicomedy
Published: London, 1952 (Athens, 1946)
Time period: 1917–1942
Setting: Crete, Greece

Themes and Issues. *Zorba the Greek* draws its tension from the relationship of two disparate souls, Zorba, a self-taught and raucous adventurer from Macedonia, and the cerebral Cretan writer he calls Boss. The dialectic between the material and intellectual nature of humanity in the struggle for spirituality is central to this work. Kazantzakis uses the theme of failure to emphasize the necessity of struggle in the creative process. Zorba and Boss both fail in repeated efforts, but from Zorba Boss learns to face this struggle with joy and pure fearlessness.

In *Zorba,* Kazantzakis deploys his knowledge of rural Cretan village culture and personalities. Kazantzakis has been criticized for his failure to develop plot and characterization in *Zorba* and for using the novel as a vehicle for his philosophy, but most readers have found his portrayal of the joyous and earthy figure of Zorba appealing.

The Plot. The narrator first encounters Alexis Zorbás in a small Piraeus café while waiting to embark for Crete to reopen a lignite mine. Boss (as he is labeled by Zorba) is a self-confessed bookworm and writer. Afraid to enter the world of action, he had demurred from accompanying his friend Stavridakis to save Greeks in the Caucasus, but now he is determined to go to Crete and involve himself in the world of affairs. The roguish Zorba convinces Boss to hire him as foreman and companion in his venture.

Upon arriving at the village in Crete, this odd couple encounters a number of colorful villagers. Zorba establishes a relationship with Dame Hortense, a dissipated French cabaret singer who has settled in the village. Boss becomes obsessed with a beautiful and lusty young widow but is unable to act on his desires. Zorba chastises his friend for sinning—by failing to satisfy the needs of this yearning woman. Zorba and Boss engage in a series of philosophical discussions that reveal the tension between the material and the intellectual world.

Under the direction of Zorba, the two begin to work the mine with laborers from the village. Zorba shows his inner strength when he risks his life to save miners during a mine shaft collapse.

The widow has also been the object of desire of a young villager, Pavlis, who drowns himself because of his unrequited love. His tragic suicide causes the villagers to ostracize the widow and his family to seek revenge against her. After Easter celebration Boss encounters the widow in the night, breaks the bonds of his fears, and consummates his love. The next morning he completes his manuscript on the Buddha. Sex with the widow has liberated Boss from his spiritual struggle on paper.

The following day, as the villagers celebrate the rebirth of Christ, the widow comes to church and is stoned. She is seized by Pavlis's relatives, but as they prepare to kill her, Zorba intervenes. Just as Zorba succeeds in overwhelming Manolakas and apparently rescuing the widow, Pavlis's father, Mavrandoni, beheads her. Rough Cretan tribal justice has been served. The widow's murder is followed by the death of Dame Hortense, whose belongings are appropriated by the villagers. She is not afforded a Christian burial because the villagers consider her a Frank—an alien beyond the embrace of Orthodoxy. Both of these locally marginalized women, sources of joy to both Zorba and Boss, are removed painfully from them.

A plan by Zorba to bring lumber down the mountain from the forest of a local monastery using a cableway is finally completed, and with villagers and monks attending the christening, the trial run results in the cableway's collapse, nearly killing the abbot. The multitude scatters leaving Boss and Zorba alone in the wake of their project's destruction. They embrace and consume the wine and lamb, and Zorba teaches Boss to dance the wild *Zéimbékiko*. Soon after, Boss and Zorba part, never to see one another again. As the novel ends, Boss has two dreams and premonitions confirmed by letters. In the first he hears his friend Stavridakis and is certain that he has died. Much later, on Aegina, he dreams of Zorba and determines to write a memorial to his friend. Upon completing it, he learns of Zorba's death in Serbia.

Analysis. As with all of Kazantzakis's novels, there is a strong element of semiautobiography in *Zorba*. However, the narrator, although constructed from shreds of Kazantzakis's life, is not the novelist. Throughout his novels Kazantzakis employs this technique of drawing upon his experience but transforming it through the writing process to something mythic, approaching legend. The action is drawn from the experiences of Kazantzakis with his real-life friend Giorgos Zorbás, with whom he had briefly operated a lignite mine in the Peloponnese in 1917. Kazantzakis maintained an occasional correspondence with Zorbás until his friend's death in 1942, and he maintained that this dynamic and earthy figure had been one of the great influences on his life. The novel represents Kazantzakis's effort to immortalize his friend and mentor. Kazantzakis uses this tale of the friendship of Zorba, the picaresque rogue, and the "quill driving" narrator

British artist Ford Madox Brown's nineteenth-century artwork *Don Juan Discovered by Haydee* (Musée d'Orsay, Paris) reflects the deep sorrow, which quickly turns to anger, expressed by the villagers over the drowning suicide of the lovesick Pavlis in Kazantzakis's novel *Zorba the Greek*.

to illustrate the philosophy he had expounded in *The Saviors of God: Spiritual Exercises*. Kazantzakis composed *Zorba* on Aegina while Greece was in the depths of famine during the German occupation. Kazantzakis's biographer and translator, Peter Bien, has argued that the novel was the author's attempt to address and identify with the tragic condition of the Greeks at that time. The novel may be read as both a philosophical and political statement.

Zorba the Greek remains Kazantzakis's most popular and widely known novel in America. It was the subject of a 1964 film of the same name directed by Michael Cacoyannis, with an original score by the celebrated Cretan composer Mikis Theodorakis. Anthony Quinn played the title role, with Alan Bates as Boss and Irene Papas as the widow.

SOURCES FOR FURTHER STUDY

Anapliotes, John. *The Real Zorbas and Nikos Kazantzakis*. Amsterdam: Adolph M. Hakkert, 1978.

Bien, Peter. "Nikos Kazantzakis's Novels on Film." *Journal of Modern Greek Studies* 19, no. 2 (2000): 161–169.

———. "*Zorba the Greek*, Nietzsche, and the Perennial Greek Predicament." *Antioch Review* (Spring 1967): 147–163.

Poulakidas, Andreas K. "Kazantzakis's *Zorba the Greek* and Nietzsche's *Thus Spake Zarathustra*." *Philological Quarterly* 49 (1970): 234–244.

Richards, Lewis A. "Fact and Fiction in Nikos Kazantzakis' *Alexis Zorbas*." *Western Humanities Review* 18 (1964): 353–359.

THE GREEK PASSION

Genre: Novel
Subgenre: Philosophical allegory
Published: New York and Athens, 1954
Time period: 1919–1920
Setting: Greek village in Anatolia

Themes and Issues. In this richly metaphoric novel Kazantzakis interweaves several eras of Greek political history with the Christian theme of death and rebirth. One small village becomes an encapsulated world in which the human quest for spirituality encounters the corruption of the common man by wealth, power, and the desires of the flesh as represented by a cast of richly framed characters. Kazantzakis's use of biblical and pre-Christian myth to provide symbols of good and evil shows that the ascending human spirit can be freed only by being reborn through eternal struggle.

The Plot. Set around 1920, *The Greek Passion* takes place in a wealthy Anatolian Greek village still under Ottoman control. Townspeople have been cast in roles for the annual Passion play. As the story progresses, each actor becomes more like the actual biblical character. Manolios, a young shepherd ready to marry, is selected as Christ. Unable to simply act the role, he assumes Christ's mission and offers his possessions to a group of poverty-stricken refugees led by the idealistic but pragmatic priest Fotis.

Christlike, Manolios offers his life to save the village elders, who have been imprisoned by the ruling Agha. His spirituality gains him followers, and he starts a revolt against the greedy leaders and the fat, rich priest, who are unwilling to share with the outcasts. They become fearful of his power, and denounced as a heretic, he is martyred by the villagers.

Analysis. The great strength of the novel is in its deep characterizations of the villagers, who are shown as complex individuals. Critics have called this novel Kazantzakis's best written and most integrated. The negative portrayal of church power upset the Greek clergy, who called for Kazantzakis's excommunication. The novel was made into the 1957 French film *Celui qui doit mourir* (He Who Must Die).

SOURCES FOR FURTHER STUDY

Bien, Peter. *Nikos Kazantzakis: Novelist. Studies in Modern Greek*. New Rochelle, NY: Aristide D. Caratzas, 1989.

Levitt, Morton P. *The Cretan Glance: The World and Art of Nikos Kazantzakis*. Columbus: Ohio State University Press, 1980.

Owens, Lewis. "Beyond Nihilism: Kazantzakis and Plotinus on the Metaphysical 'One' That Does Not Exist." *Journal of Modern Greek Studies* 19, no. 2 (2001): 269–281.

THE LAST TEMPTATION OF CHRIST

Genre: Novel
Subgenre: Philosophical allegory
Published: New York, 1960 (Athens, 1955)
Time period: Time of Christ
Setting: Biblical Galilee and Judea

Themes and Issues. Kazantzakis's best-known and most controversial novel after *Zorba the Greek*, *The Last Temptation of Christ* draws upon the mythic stories of the Old and New Testament to re-create the struggle of a human Christ overcoming sensual temptation with spirituality. Every incident comes from the Bible, but each is changed so as to reject a narrow interpretation of God and replace it with a Christ who is not reborn but dies as a man for the sake of all humanity.

The Plot. Jesus of Nazareth is an ordinary carpenter who builds crosses for the Romans. Suffering from epileptic fits, he struggles to accept God's will. After facing many temptations, he realizes he is the Messiah. Disciples gather around him to accompany him as he preaches love and performs miracles. The last and greatest temptation takes place as Jesus is crucified. An angel appears and takes him to a simple village, where he marries, has children, and lives like any man until he forces himself awake. Rejecting the pleasure of a normal life and the immortality of family, he accepts his role and dies victorious.

Analysis. This crucifixion denies a limited role for mankind. Divinity is seen as something in reach of everyone who perseveres and overcomes temptations. Jesus is no different from other men in whom body and soul coexist in constant tension. There is also the tension between the political and spiritual. The people want a political messiah who will free them from the Romans, but Jesus offers spiritual salvation and the knowledge that the world can renew itself instead.

This is Kazantzakis's only modernist narrative featuring subjective time and an ambiguous point of view. The book drew the wrath of both Orthodox and Catholic authorities, who viewed the "humanizing" of Christ as sacrilege or distortion or both. Martin Scorsese's 1988 film adaptation did not receive a friendly reception from a great many Christian groups in the United States.

SOURCES FOR FURTHER STUDY

Antonakes, Michael. "Christ, Kazantzakis, and Controversy in Greece." *Modern Greek Studies Yearbook* 6 (1990): 331–343.

Bien, Peter. *Tempted by Happiness: Kazantzakis' Post-Christian Christ.* Wallingford, PA: Pendle Hill Publications, 1984.

Chilson, Richard. "The Christ of Nikos Kazantzakis." *Thought* 47 (1972): 69–89.

Iannone, Carol. "*The Last Temptation* Reconsidered." *First Things* (February 1996): 50–54.

Levitt, Morton P. "The Modernist Kazantzakis and *The Last Temptation of Christ.*" *Mosaic* 6, no. 2 (1973): 103–124.

Petrolle, Jean Ellen "Nikos Kazantzakis and *The Last Temptation*: Irony and Dialectic in a Spiritual Ontology of Body." *Journal of Modern Greek Studies* 11, no. 2 (1993): 273.

Other Works

THE ODYSSEY: A MODERN SEQUEL (1938). Kazantzakis viewed *The Odyssey*, an epic poem of 33,333 lines on which he labored through eight drafts, as his masterwork. The English title was proposed by the translator, Kimon Friar, and it suggests that this massive poem must be placed among the writings of other giants of twentieth-century modernist literature such as D. H. Lawrence, James Joyce, and Thomas Mann.

Kazantzakis began the composition of his modern *Odyssey* in 1925 on Crete, three years after the publication of James Joyce's *Ulysses*, and completed it in 1938 on Aegina. Into this massive work he poured his encyclopedic knowledge of archaeology, myth, and literature and his love for Homer (Kazantzakis had translated Homer into demotic Greek), as well as experience culled from his personal odyssey. It is in many ways semiautobiographical, although Kazantzakis uses this quintessential Greek hero who challenges the rules of society and the cosmos in the same picaresque mode later employed in *Zorba*. Once again, Kazantzakis describes the journey of a hero who confronts the existential challenge, fearlessly staring death in the eye but knowing that he is without hope.

ST. FRANCIS (1956). The life of Saint Francis of Assisi allows Kazantzakis to delve into the relationship between politics and religion. Francis's ability to turn political failure into spiritual victory is the main theme of the novel. The narrator, Brother Leo, provides an earthy

Kazantzakis expresses his love for Homer, seen here in artist Mattia Preti's seventeenth-century painting *Homer,* in illustrious fashion in what he considered his masterwork, the 1938 epic poem *The Odyssey: A Modern Sequel.*

view of Francis's transformation from a wealthy merchant's son to a beloved but fierce opponent of injustice.

Francis is struck ill with a vision that convinces him to follow God's path. He must face many temptations and trials on his journey to rebuild his spiritual faith. He begins the journey by rejecting potential happiness, reputation, and wealth and wanders about preaching universal love.

He then rebuilds a tiny church, which represents the reestablishment of faith. Joined by 12 disciples, his new order is riven by dissension. Kazantzakis uses this incident to express his own frustration with Greek political factionalism. Francis abdicates and goes to Egypt to convert the sultan but again fails.

He returns home and takes up his quest again. By rigidly adhering to his personal doctrine, he succeeds where before he failed, because it is only by acting as if one is immortal that death is conquered. St. Francis accomplishes Kazantzakis's dream—the triumph of spirit over flesh.

FREEDOM OR DEATH (1953). *Freedom or Death*, the most historical of Kazantzakis's novels, portrays the unsuccessful Cretan rebellion of 1889. It is not a wholly accurate historical representation but rather a conflation of the numerous nineteenth-century Cretan rebellions against Turkish domination. Once again, Kazantzakis uses the novel form to spin a legend of mythic proportions. He compares the condition of the Cretan people under Turkish oppression to that of Christ on the cross. The metaphor of a people recrucified but renewing their struggle echoes the themes of *The Greek Passion*. This epic of futile resistance against overwhelming odds again employs Kazantzakis's key metaphor, the "Cretan glance." Here it is applied to its source, the *pallikária* of his native island, who confront life and death with equanimity.

The protagonists are Kapetán Mihális, a protypical *pallikári*, and Nuri Bey, the Turkish ruler of Megalokastro, who is portrayed sympathetically. Their mutual respect has led them to become blood brothers. Mihális, however, is smitten by Eminé, Nuri Bey's Circassian mistress, and will ultimately kidnap her and lead a rebellion and die heroically, facing the Turks with the war cry "Freedom or Death!" in his throat.

Kazantzakis was severely criticized by Greek nationalists for his violent portrayal of the Cretan resistance and for his depiction of the Church, and once again calls for his excommunication resulted.

THE FRATRICIDES (1963). Kazantzakis's last novel, *The Fratricides,* is set in Castello, a mountain village in Epirus during the 1946–1949 Greek civil war. Its protagonist, Father Yánaros, struggles futilely to bring peace between the blackhoods (monarchists) defending the village and the redhoods (communists) who lay siege from the encircling mountains. The redhood leader, Captain Drakos, is Father Yánaros's son. Castello is defended by a captain who had been Drakos's brother-in-arms. As in *Freedom or Death,* these "brothers in conflict" are unified by their love for the captain's wife, who abandons the captain for Drakos. The action is set during Easter week, and the battle over the village once again uses the metaphor of Christ's Passion to symbolize the human struggle for spiritual freedom. Father Yánaros refuses to allow the villagers to resurrect Christ without the participation of the rebels and negotiates the surrender of Castello to Drakos, who promises not to exact revenge. Upon entering the village, however, this pledge is broken, and the novel ends with the Christlike Yánaros's execution.

Written at the end of the fratricidal struggle that led to Kazantzakis's exile and published posthumously, *The Fratricides* has been criticized as an imperfect work. It does, however, offer insight into Kazantzakis's views on the war and on his politics.

Resources

Most major collections of Kazantzakis's manuscripts are located in Greece. Institutions and organizations of interest to students of Nikos Kazantzakis and his work include the following:

Kazantzakis Museum. Located on Crete in the village of Varvári, or Myrtia, 20 kilometers south of Iráklion next to Kazantzakis's father's house, this museum also holds an important archive of Kazantzakis manuscripts and personal effects. The museum maintains a Web site (http://www.interkriti.org/culture/kazantzakis/kazmus.htm). A link to information on this museum is located at the Web site at the Historical Museum of Crete.

Société des Amis de Nikos Kazantzaki (Society of Friends of Nikos Kazantzakis). Although this is an international francophone organization of Kazantzakis enthusiasts, it is still an important organization for any student of the author. It publishes the semiannual *Le regard crétois: Revue de la société des amis de N. Kazantzaki.*

Society of Cretan Historical Studies. This important historical organization maintains the principal archive of Kazantzakis manuscripts and personal effects at the Historical Museum of Crete in Iráklion. The museum has reconstructed the Kazantzakis library and study as they were in Kazantzakis's residence in exile at Antibes, France. The museum maintains a very valuable and useful Web site—the official Nikos Kazantzakis Homepage (http://www.historical-museum.gr/kazantzakis/). This site commemorates the 40th anniversary of Kazantzakis's death and includes a rich variety of photos, letters, biographical materials, bibliography, press clippings, and recorded interviews with Kazantzakis. It includes Peter Bien's detailed chronology of Kazantzakis's life and work. This is the most accessible and useful initial site for students interested in the author.

HAROLD A. KOSTER

Index

Page numbers in **boldface** type indicate article titles. Page numbers in *italic* type indicate illustrations.